AIR CAMPAIGN

PLOESTI 1943

The great raid on Hitler's Romanian oil refineries

STEVEN J. ZALOGA ILLUSTRATED BY STEVE NOON

OSPREY PUBLISHING
Bloomsbury Publishing Plc
PO Box 883, Oxford, OX1 9PL, UK
1385 Broadway, 5th Floor, New York, NY 10018, USA
E-mail: info@ospreypublishing.com
www.ospreypublishing.com

OSPREY is a trademark of Osprey Publishing Ltd

First published in Great Britain in 2019

A catalog record for this book is available from the British Library.

ISBN: PB 9781472831804; eBook 9781472831972;
ePDF 9781472831965; XML 9781472831958

19 20 21 22 23   10 9 8 7 6 5 4 3 2 1

Maps by Bounford.com
3D BEVs by Paul Kime
Diagram by Adam Tooby
Index by Alison Worthington
Typeset by PDQ Digital Media Solutions, Bungay, UK
Printed and bound in India by Replika Press Private Ltd.

Osprey Publishing supports the Woodland Trust, the UK's leading woodland conservation charity.

To find out more about our authors and books visit www.ospreypublishing.com. Here you will find extracts, author interviews, details of forthcoming events and the option to sign up for our newsletter.

Author's Note
The author would especially like to thank Wojciech Łuczak, Richard Griffith, and Dana Bell for help in providing material for this book. Unless otherwise noted, all photos in this book are from US government sources including the National Archives and Records Administration II at College Park, Maryland, and the Library of Congress in Washington, DC.
In this book, the city of Ploieşti is referred to by its more common English name, Ploesti; likewise Bucharest. The USAAF bases in the Benghazi area were on Mediterranean time, which was GMT + 3 hours. The German and Romanian units used German/Eastern European time, which was GMT + 2 hours. The USAAF used Greenwich Mean Time for its official reports, and this time is used in this book.

Glossary

AAA	Antiaircraft artillery
av.	Aviator (Romanian)
BVS	*Bulgarski voennovozdushni sili*: Bulgarian Air Force
CAA	*Comandamentul Apărării Antiaeriene*: Air Defense Command
CCS	Combined Chiefs of Staff
Chi-Stelle	*Chiffrierstelle, Oberbefehlshaber der Luftwaffe*: Signals intelligence service of Luftwaffe high command
Esc. Vt.	*Escadrila Vânătoare*: Romanian Fighter Squadron
FARR	*Forţele Aeriene Regale Române*: Royal Romanian Air Force
HALPRO	Halverson Project
HMG	heavy machine gun
IP	Initial Point
Jäfu	*Jagdfliegerführer*: Fighter Control
JG	*Jagdgeschwader*: German Fighter Squadron
NATO	North African Theater of Operations
NJG	*Nachtjagdgeschwader*: German Night-fighter Squadron
Por.	*Poruchik* (Bulgarian): Lieutenant
USSTAF	United States Strategic Air Force
W-Leit	*Wetterleit Stellen* (Weather Station); Covername for Luftwaffe signals intelligence units

CONTENTS

INTRODUCTION 4

CHRONOLOGY 8

ATTACKER'S CAPABILITIES 9

DEFENDERS' CAPABILITIES 14

CAMPAIGN OBJECTIVES 30

THE CAMPAIGN 38

ANALYSIS 77

FURTHER READING 92

INDEX 95

INTRODUCTION

Ploesti was the center of the Romanian petroleum industry, responsible for about 85 percent of Romania's refined oil products.

Oil is the lifeblood of the modern war machine. Warplanes, tanks, and warships all require a constant supply of fuel. Nazi Germany had no significant oil deposits and its only domestic source was the expensive and complicated conversion of coal into synthetic fuels. This could only provide about a third of its fuel requirements. Germany needed to import the rest. Through the summer of 1941, Germany obtained oil on the foreign market, from captured supplies, and from deliveries by its erstwhile ally, the Soviet Union. In view of Hitler's intentions to invade the Soviet Union, other sources were needed. The five main oil producers in 1941 were the USA, USSR, Venezuela, Iran, and Romania. The first four sources were unavailable, and Berlin turned its attention to Romania. Through diplomatic pressure, Romania was gradually brought into the German orbit. In November 1940, Romania formally allied itself to Berlin. About 85 percent of Romania's oil was refined near the town of Ploesti in the Prahova valley north of the capital city of Bucharest. Not surprisingly, the Allies viewed Ploesti as a prime target for attack as a means to strangle Germany's vital supply of fuel.

Operation *Tidal Wave*, the US Army Air Force raid on the Ploesti oil refineries on August 1, 1943, was one of the most controversial missions of World War II. The imposing distance between Allied airfields on the Mediterranean and central Romania delayed a large-scale mission until the summer of 1943. The results of *Tidal Wave* were disappointing and the costs were high. Of the 178 B-24 heavy bombers taking part in the mission, 54 bombers were lost, 55 seriously damaged, and aircrew casualties were over five hundred men. Ploesti's refineries were back in production within a month. Sobered by this experience, the US Army Air Force did not return to attack the Ploesti oil complex until the spring of 1944.

Early attacks on Ploesti

Tidal Wave was not the first attack on Ploesti. Allied interest in attacking Ploesti predated American actions, with British and French plans dating back as early as the 1940 campaign. These 1939–40 schemes mainly involved sabotage of the refineries or blockage of the Danube river oil shipment routes. The Director of Naval Intelligence in London, in conjunction with the naval attaché in Bucharest, organized a half-baked attempt in March–April 1940 to block key points on the Danube. One scheme involved sinking barges in the narrows at the Iron Gates. In the event, none of these operations had the least success. In November 1940, Churchill demanded a new plan to attack Ploesti from the air. RAF chief of air staff, Air Chief Marshal Sir Cyril Newall, presented a plan involving five bomber squadrons, dropping 258 tons of bombs monthly over four months that would achieve 25–30 percent destruction of the Ploesti refineries. The German conquest of Greece in April 1940 put an end to these plans since no other airfields available to the RAF at the time were in range.

The first air strikes on the Ploesti oil fields were conducted by Soviet bomber units in the summer of 1941 following the start of Germany's Operation *Barbarossa* invasion. An initial strike was conducted on June 26, 1941 by 17 aircraft. Only about half the aircraft reached the target area and results were negligible. On July 9, the General Staff of the Red Army ordered a coordinated attack on Romanian oil fields by the army air force (VVS-RKKA) and the navy's air forces. These missions were conducted primarily by the 2nd Air Force of the Black Sea Fleet and the 21st and 81st Air Forces of the 4th Air Corps flying from Crimea and other bases around the Black Sea.

The threat of Romanian and German fighters forced the use of night attacks. A total of 13 night raids were conducted from July 3 to July 22, mainly by naval DB-3F bombers. Returning air crews reported that large fires had been initiated during the raids. In fact, most of the attacks were wasted on dummy refineries created by Luftwaffe camouflage specialists as detailed below.

The single most successful raid took place on July 13, 1941 when six Pe-2 bombers of the 5th Squadron, 40th Bomber Regiment of the Black Sea Fleet under Capt Aleksandr P. Tsurtsumiy staged a daytime raid on Ploesti from a forward base in Moldova. Soviet accounts claim that the attack destroyed 202 fuel tanks, 46 oil tanks, and two warehouses along with 220,000 tons of oil products, which was a substantial exaggeration. Four bombs hit the Astra Română refinery and three at Lumina. However, 15 bombs landed on the Orion refinery, striking a large tank park, an oil plant, and putting the Orion facility out of use until November 1941. A Luftwaffe report indicated that a total of five large storage tanks and six small tanks were set on fire, 17 railroad tank cars were destroyed and 29 damaged.

One of the more unusual Soviet aircraft used in the summer 1941 attacks on Romania was the Zveno-SPB (Sostavnoi Pikiruyuschiy Bombardirovschik – Combination Dive Bomber). This consisted of a TB-3-4AM-34FRN bomber carrying two Polikarpov I-16 Tip 24 fighter-bombers as parasites under the wings. Six of these were deployed with Shubikov's Circus, the 2nd Special Squadron of the 32nd IAP (Fighter Regiment) of the 62nd Aviation Brigade of the Black Sea Fleet Air Force based at Yevpatoria in Crimea. The first of the missions was on June 26, 1941 against the Constanţa oil depot.

About 20,000 metric tons of gasoline and crude oil burned. The fires blazed for two nights and caused damage estimated as Lei 200 million ($1 million).

The refinery attacks proved to be ineffective and, as a result, the Soviet air attacks shifted to attacks against key bridges and transport facilities associated with the oil industry. The air attacks into Romania continued into September 1941, but declined sharply afterwards as the *Wehrmacht* pushed eastward. According to Soviet accounts, Soviet bomber formations in June–November 1941 conducted 92 raids on Romania dropping 11,425 bombs totaling 75.3 metric tons. The Luftwaffe recorded 32 raids, dropping 542 bombs, in the Ploesti area. Luftwaffe and Romanian fighters claimed to have shot down 81 Soviet bombers during this campaign. In August 1941, Hitler directed the *Wehrmacht* to speed up its capture of Crimea, one of the main reasons being the threat it posed to Romanian oil supplies.

HALPRO mission

B-24D "Ripper 1st" (41-11614) was one of the original 23 HALPRO B-24s that later formed the basis for the 376th Group. It served with the 515th Squadron but did not take part in *Tidal Wave*.

The first and most obscure American mission against Ploesti from the Mediterranean was conducted in June 1942. A small task force of 23 B-24D bombers codenamed HALPRO (Halverson Project) was formed under the command of Col Harry Halverson. This was intended as a reprise of the Doolittle raid against Japan, but from the opposite direction. The plan was to fly from Florida to China via Brazil, Africa, and the Middle East. HALPRO would operate from China, flying bomber missions against Japan. HALPRO departed the United States on May 22, 1942 for Khartoum, Sudan, and flew on to northeast Egypt. By this

time, a Japanese army offensive threatened the intended bomber base in Chekiang, China. As a result, the Army Air Force Planning Division changed the mission to an impromptu attack on Ploesti.

When the mission was launched on the night of June 11, 1942 from Fayid, Egypt, only 13 B-24D bombers were serviceable. Halverson instructed his crews to fly directly to Romania, and to return to Habbaniyah, Iraq. One crew became detached and bombed the Romanian port of Constanța. The other 12 Liberators made single approaches to Ploesti at 10,000–14,000ft during daylight on June 12, 1942. HALPRO dropped 24 tons of bombs, but cloud cover and navigational problems prevented any precision in the attack. Only six bombs impacted near Ploesti, destroying three houses, killing three civilians and wounding three others. Constanța was more heavily hit with 11 bombs, and a variety of small towns and villages suffered a handful of explosions. Both Romanian and German fighters were scrambled and pilot av. Vasile Pascu of the Grupul 8 claimed to have shot down one of the bombers. B-24D "Town Hall," piloted by Lt Frederick Nesbitt, was damaged during an air attack, but landed safely in Turkey.

Four bombers landed at Habbaniyah, five landed at other fields in Iraq and Syria, and four were interned in neutral Turkey. The first Ploesti mission by the USAAF was poorly planned and had completely insufficient resources. It would take a year before it was repeated.

The crew of B-24D (41-11593) "Black Mariah II" piloted by Lt John W. Kidd was one of the original Halverson Project bombers and subsequently became part of the 513th Squadron, 376th Group. The aircraft and crew were lost on a night mission near Crete on October 29–30, 1942.

CHRONOLOGY

1941
June 26 First Soviet air strike on Ploesti

July 13 Most destructive of the Soviet raids conducted on Ploesti by naval Pe-2 bombers

1942
June 12 HALPRO raid on Ploesti

May 13 Trident Conference tentatively approves *Tidal Wave*

1943
June 5 Gen Dwight Eisenhower, NATO Commander-in-Chief, approves *Tidal Wave*

August 1, 1943
0400 First *Tidal Wave* aircraft take off from Benghazi

0530 *Tidal Wave* force heads over the Mediterranean towards the Greek coast near Corfu

0855 *Tidal Wave* force passes Corfu in the Ionian Sea heading for Albanian coast

0930 *Tidal Wave* passes Albanian-Serbian border between Pogradec and Tsarev Dvor

0955 *Tidal Wave* passes over St Jovan

1025 Bulgarian 6th Fighter Regiment scrambles three fighters to intercept *Tidal Wave*

1055 Romanian barrage balloon and smoke battalions alerted

1111 Second formation crosses Romanian frontier

1115 5.Flak-Division puts German-Romanian Flak batteries on alert

1118 Romanian fighter squadrons scrambled for intercepts over Ploesti

1120 I./JG.4 squadrons scrambled for intercepts over Ploesti

1129 Second formation passes Craiova

1135 The 376th and 93rd Groups arrive over 1st IP (Initial Point) of Piteşti

1145 The 376th and 93rd Groups pass over 2nd IP at Târgovişte and make a wrong turn

1145 Jäfu Rumänien alerts fighters that bombers are approaching at low altitude

1150 First contact between Grupul 6 and 376th Group over Săbăreni

1150 The 93rd Group breaks formation and heads toward Ploesti

1155 Second Formation reaches 1st IP at Piteşi; 389th Group heads for Câmpina

1155 The 376th Group turns away from Bucharest and back to Ploesti

1155 The 93rd Group begins bombing refineries along southeastern side of Ploesti

1200 First Luftwaffe interception of the day, southwest of Ploesti

1205 98th Group and 44th Group arrive at 3rd IP over Floreşti and make the turn for Ploesti

1213 98th Group and 44th Group bomb their assigned Target White refineries

1213 The 389th Group strikes Target Red

1215 The elements of 44th Group led by Lt Col Jim Posey attack Target Blue

1244 Last Luftwaffe interception of *Tidal Wave* bomber in the Ploesti area

1400 Bulgarian 6th Fighter Regiment begins intercepts of returning *Tidal Wave* bombers

1530 JG.27 begins interceptions of returning *Tidal Wave* bombers near Kefalonia on the Ionian Sea

1713 Final interception of a *Tidal Wave* bomber over the Mediterranean by JG.27

1720 First bombers return to Benghazi

ATTACKER'S CAPABILITIES
XI Bomber Command in North Africa

B-24D (41-11591) "Lorraine" of the 513th Squadron, 376th Group, piloted by Lt William Zimmerman, is seen here splashing through "Lake Manduria," an area flooded by a recent rainfall at one of the bases near Benghazi. This aircraft served with the original HALPRO detachment when it was known as "Queen Bee."

As detailed below, the *Tidal Wave* plan had a requirement for five heavy bombardment groups. Two of these were already in the North African Theater of Operations (NATO). The 376th Heavy Bombardment Group, commanded by Col Keith K. Compton, had grown out of the earlier Halverson Detachment and still included aircraft and crews who had flown the original 1942 mission. The 98th Heavy Bombardment Group, commanded by Lt Col John "Killer" Kane, had arrived in North Africa later in the summer of 1942. Both of these groups had seen extensive combat and were familiar with operating conditions in the Mediterranean theater.

The two desert commanders had strained personal relations that complicated the execution of Operation *Tidal Wave*. "K. K." Compton was a by-the-book commander, and a team-player who was well liked by the senior USAAF commanders in the Mediterranean theater. "Killer" Kane's nickname stemmed from a comic book character in the "Flash Gordon" series, and not from any particular bloody-mindedness. He was a charismatic but abrasive leader and showed particular disdain for "experts" from Washington who had not seen extensive combat experience on the B-24 bomber. Their differences in command style eventually erupted over the issue of flying techniques, as is described in more detail below.

The low-altitude tactics for the Ploesti mission were first demonstrated by the 201st Provisional Combat Wing in Britain. The commander of this formation, Col E. J. Timberlake, was instrumental in the training regimen for the Ploesti mission. It was the three heavy bombardment groups from this wing that were transferred from the Eighth Air Force in Britain to the IX Bomber Command in Libya for *Tidal Wave*.

The three groups flew to Libya from Britain in late June 1943.

The 44th Heavy Bombardment Group had seen its combat debut in November 1942 and by early March 1943 had lost 13 of its original 27 B-24s. During the May 14, 1943 mission on the German submarine base at Kiel, the 44th lost five of its 17 B-24s and its gunners were credited with having shot down 21 German fighters. The 44th was awarded a Distinguished Unit Citation for its conduct on this mission. The group left Britain for Libya on June 27.

Leading *Tidal Wave* aboard the B-24D command ship "Teggie Ann" was the 386th Group commander, Col K. K. Compton to the left and leader of IX Bomber Command, Brig Gen Uzal Ent to the right.

B-24D (42-72843) flew with the 512th Squadron, 376th Group but did not take part in the August 1, 1943 *Tidal Wave* mission. It is the best-known B-24D, preserved at the National Museum of the US Air Force at Wright-Patterson AFB, Dayton, Ohio.

The 93rd Group had seen its combat debut on October 9, 1942 attacking factories near Lille, France. It spent much of the fall of 1942 attacking German U-boat pens on the Bay of Biscay on the French Atlantic coast. A large detachment from the group was sent to North Africa in December 1942, receiving a Distinguished Unit Citation for operations in that theater. The detachment returned to England in late February 1943 and continued missions in France, the Low Countries, and Germany. The 93rd Group departed the UK on June 26.

The 389th Group was new and inexperienced, departing the UK last on July 2. All five groups were equipped with the B-24D Liberator heavy bomber, but the 389th Group had received a later production series fitted with a ball turret in the belly. Since this had different handling characteristics, this group was assigned a mission slightly separate from the other

B-24D "Wash's Tub" (41-11636), served with the 514th Squadron, 376th Group at Ploesti, piloted by Lt James Bock. It survived 73 missions and is seen here in September 1943 when sent back to the United States for a bond drive.

groups, attacking the refinery in Câmpina north of Ploesti. In the event, the ball turrets were removed prior to *Tidal Wave* to reduce weight and drag and permit greater range since underbelly defense was not a high priority on a low-level mission.

Prior to the Ploesti mission, the five groups conducted 1,183 sorties in support of Operation *Husky* in July 1943. During these missions, 18 aircraft were lost, including ten in combat. The last of these was a mission on Rome on July 19, after which the groups were sequestered for training for the Ploesti mission.

In late March 1943, Lt Norman Appold of the 376th Group suggested using low-altitude tactics to deal with the reinforced concrete train sheds on the Gulf of Messina on Sicily that had proven impervious to previous attacks from normal altitudes. Col K. K. Compton, the group commander, approved the mission to help gain experience in low-altitude tactics. This attack took place on the night of March 29–30. In the event, low overcast obscuring the target prevented the intended attack, but the secondary target of the rail yards at Crotone were successfully bombed. In the wake of this raid, Lt Brian Flavelle suggested a twilight raid to avoid the early morning mists that had foiled Appold's attacks. This was conducted on April 1, 1943 with Flavelle leading the attack in the lead aircraft "Wash's Tub." These two small-scale raids gave the lead *Tidal Wave* group some confidence that the Liberator could be used in low-level attacks.

A close-up of the nose of "Lorraine" showing the two machine guns added as forward armament on some of the *Tidal Wave* B-24D for Flak suppression.

The *Tidal Wave* training program in late July 1943 was intended to show that large formations could safely conduct a mission at low altitude. The training regime was aimed at preparing the five Liberator groups to safely conduct the low-altitude attack while placing as many aircraft over the target in the shortest amount of time possible to minimize losses to enemy air defenses. Individual crews were expected to be able to drop bombs from 300ft (90m) with a maximum circular error of no more than 100ft (30m). A training target was erected in the desert near Soluch, Libya. Training began on Tuesday, July 20 with briefings, followed by

Due to the importance of *Tidal Wave*, the Ninth Air Force installed numerous cameras in the bombers to record battle damage. Here, Capt Jesse Sabin of an USAAF Combat Camera unit makes a final inspection of a camera mounted in the bombardier's position in one of the B-24D bombers.

practice missions by single aircraft, 6-ship formations, and 12-ship formations. One of the crew members later recounted that:

> We ran approximately 12 missions over the replica of the oil fields, approaching, attacking, and departing exactly as we intended doing on the actual raid. Each element was given a specific dummy target … and we practiced until we could bomb it in our sleep. When we finally did get over Ploesti, our movements were almost automatic.

The training program was nearly derailed by the widespread outbreak of amoebic dysentery among the aircrews and ground crews who at the time were living in very primitive desert conditions. Although the worst of the outbreak had abated by the time of the mission, a significant number of the crews were still weakened from the aftereffects of the infection at the time of the mission.

On July 28 and July 29, the entire task force participated in a gigantic mock attack mission, bombing the dummy targets with 100lb practice bombs in a two-minute assault. Besides the training missions, an extensive program of briefings was conducted. Five large models of the target area were prepared with RAF assistance including 1:50,000 scale models of Ploesti, Brazi, and Câmpina. Special navigational aids were provided to each navigator including detailed map references along with photographs and sketches of the main check points along the route to provide explicit visual cues. Each crew received their own target folder that included target map sheets and perspective drawings of their targets at the refineries. The bombardiers were provided with special illustrations of their specific aim points. It was the most carefully prepared USAAF heavy bomber mission to date.

Capping the preparation was a special 45-minute film that provided an overview of the mission, detailed information for pilots and navigators, and finally a portion devoted to the bombardiers. A later USAAF report summarized the message of the film: The job was tough, although by no means impossible. The mission's importance justified the risk.

The original plans assumed that the mission would be led by the Ninth Air Force commander, Maj Gen Lewis Brereton, and would include other key officers such as Col Jacob Smart and Col Edward J. Timberlake. In the event, USAAF chief Hap Arnold sent explicit instructions days before the mission that Brereton, Smart, and Timberlake would not take part in the mission since they were all privy to a broad range of top-secret information that could not be put at risk. As a result, Brig Gen Uzal Ent, the head of IX Bomber Command, would lead the mission.

Aside from the crew training, the IX Bomber Command undertook a Herculean maintenance effort on the aircraft. At the start of the training period, 191 aircraft were available but only 131 were operational. The main problem was a shortage of engines since the average time between overhauls for the engines was only 200 hours. After additional aircraft were flown in, and new engines provided, IX Bomber Command had 193 B-24D bombers ready on July 31 out of the 202 on hand.

The main disagreement between group commanders Compton and Kane was over the matter of the optimum flying method for the B-24 bomber. Compton listened to outside experts who advised flying the B-24D on the mission at a high speed to gain optimum lift from the bomber's Davis wing design. Kane disagreed with this flying technique, arguing that too many of his bombers were suffering from the abrasive desert conditions which resulted in low engine life and high oil consumption. Kane's group was based deeper in the Libyan desert exacerbating this problem, while Compton's was nearer the coast. Kane recommended a more cautious application of speed on the approach to Ploesti to minimize bombers aborting the mission due to mechanical problems. In the event, the senior commanders such as Brereton and Ent did not step in and settle the matter, and this dispute remained simmering in the background.

The B-24D Liberators had two major modifications for *Tidal Wave*. A portion of the aircraft leading the formations had additional .50cal heavy machine guns added in the nose for strafing Flak batteries. In addition, all aircraft received two jettisonable 400-gallon "Tokyo" tanks in their bomb-bay to extend their effective range. Some aircraft also had armor plate added, mostly taken from crashed Allied and Axis fighters.

The bomb loads of the individual aircraft were tailored to their specific targets. All bombs were fitted with delay fuzes since the bombs were dropped from such low altitudes. Of the 1,000lb bombs, most were fitted with one-hour delay fuzes but two dozen had one- to six-hour delay fuzes. The 500lb bombs were mostly fitted with 45-second delay fuzes, but about a quarter had longer delays. The long-delay fuzes were intended to discourage fire-fighters. Many aircraft were issued with boxes of small British incendiary thermite bombs that were carried near the waist gun positions for the gunners to throw out when passing over the targets.

IX Bomber Command Heavy Bombardment Groups, Operation *Tidal Wave*				
Group	**Commander**	**Nickname**	**Target**	**Operational strength**
376th BG	Col Keith Compton	Liberandos	White I	29
93rd BG	Lt Col Addison Baker	Flying Circus	White II, III	39
98th BG	Lt Col John Kane	Pyramiders	White IV	47
44th BG	Col Leon Johnson	Flying 8-Balls	White V, Blue	37
389th BG	Col Jack Wood	Sky Scorpions	Red	26

DEFENDERS' CAPABILITIES
Guarding the black gold

The barrage balloon barrier around Ploesti accounted for at least four B-24D bombers during the *Tidal Wave* raid and damaged many more. The standard German type was the 200m^3 Sperrballone, so designated by the volume of hydrogen contained. The original barrier around Ploesti was established by the Luftwaffe but, in October 1942, the Germans turned over responsibility to the Romanian 3rd Balloon Battalion.

Germany's dependence on Romanian oil after the June 1941 invasion of the Soviet Union prompted Berlin's intense interest in the defense of the Ploesti oil refineries. Romania's defensive capabilities were quite modest, even after the May 27, 1940 "oil-for-arms" treaty that pledged a steady stream of German weapons in return for Romanian oil. The September 1940 coup by Gen Ion Antonescu set the stage for closer German-Romanian military cooperation, and the following month, the Luftwaffe began to deploy a special Luftwaffe mission to Romania to improve the air defense situation.

Romanian AAA defense

The Romanian army slowly modernized its antiaircraft artillery (AAA) forces through the 1930s, though within the crippling constraints of a threadbare defense budget. On July 1, 1930, the Air Defense Command (CAA: Comandamentul Apărării Antiaeriene) was formed to accelerate the modernization of national air defense. By the late 1930s, Romania had a very modest force of 18 antiaircraft artillery (AAA) batteries equipped mainly with machine guns and small numbers of antiaircraft guns. There were only three fixed site AAA batteries in Bucharest with old French 75mm M1897 guns and one battery each in Braşov and Galaţi with the Škoda 76mm gun. In April 1940, the Prahova valley, including Ploesti, was defended by seven AAA guns, ten 13.2mm machine guns, 132 8mm machine guns, and a single searchlight battery. There were also three fighter squadrons assigned to defense of the oil region.

In 1938–40, efforts were made to improve the situation with new imports.

In 1939, the CAA was reorganized to unify air defense artillery, air defense fighter squadrons, and associated command-and-control networks. The three zones were designated as Air Region I Iasi (Regiunea I Aeriană Iasi), Air Region II Cluj, and Air Region III Bucharest; Ploesti was part of the Bucharest zone. Further centralization was undertaken on October 28, 1940 when the Air Defense Command was assigned not only the national AAA regiments and air defense regions, but also territorial defense forces and the Passive Defense Service (Apărării Pasive). In February 1941, following the arrival of the first Luftwaffe Flak units, the joint Comandamentul Militar al Regiuii Petrolifere (Military Command of the Petroleum District) was organized under the command of Gen Vintilă Davidescu. This included various border guard, gendarme, and local defense units, as well as antiaircraft artillery. Overall command of the Ploesti Flak force was under Oberst Adolf Gerlach who headed the original Flak Lehr Regiment (Flak Training Regiment) that later became Flak-Regiment.180. Under his command was a Romanian AAA group under Lt Col Gheorghe Turtureanu that at the time included two battalions with seven 75mm batteries and a 13mm HMG battery.

By the summer of 1941, the Romanian air defense force had been expanded to nine antiaircraft gun regiments with 691 AAA guns. A portion of these antiaircraft regiments were assigned to the field army, but three regimental-sized air defense groups (Grupările antiaeriene) were created, named after their basing areas: Bucharest, Moldova, and Şiret. Ploesti fell within the Bucharest zone. The performance of Romanian antiaircraft batteries against Soviet raids in 1941 was mixed. The lack of modern fire controls and radar direction led to heavy wastage of precious stocks of expensive ammunition. Efforts were underway to license produce the Rheinmetall 37mm and Vickers 75mm guns at the Reşiţa and Astra-Braşov factories as well as associated ammunition. Even as late as 1942, Romania's air defense equipment was completely inadequate, as revealed by this Luftwaffe assessment.

Romanian Flak Equipment, 1942	
Hotchkiss 13.2mm HMG	200
Oerlikon 20mm	45
Hotchkiss 25mm Mod. 30	75
Rheinmetall 37mm Mod. 18	184
Bofors 40mm	75
French 75mm M1897 semi-fixed	12
French 75mm M1897 self-propelled	16
Russian 76mm Gun	8
Vickers 75mm Mod. 32	112
Škoda 76mm Mod. 25	4

To accelerate the modernization of the Romanian air defense forces in the Prahova/Ploesti region, in January 1942 the Luftwaffe agreed to transfer some of its antiaircraft equipment to Romanian crews. As a result, by the summer of 1942, the Romanian Ploesti defenses had been expanded to three machine gun batteries, 12 20mm batteries, two 37mm batteries, two 75mm Vickers batteries, 18 88mm batteries, and two searchlight batteries. In addition to these new weapons, the Romanian batteries were linked into the German fire control networks. By the summer of 1943, the Romanian national air defense units included 66 heavy AAA batteries, 55 light AAA batteries, 14 machine gun batteries, ten searchlight batteries, and three captive balloon batteries.

At the time of the August 1943 *Tidal Wave* attack, the Romanian AAA forces in the vicinity of Ploesti consisted of the 5th Air Defense Brigade (Brigada 5 Artilerie Antiaeriană), commanded by Col Ion Rudeanu. This included two regiments, the 7th AAA Regiment (Regimentul 7 Artilerie Antiaeriană) and the 9th AAA Regiment. These two regiments were deployed to supplement their German Flakgruppe counterparts. The 7th AAA Regiment deployed as part of Flakgruppe Ploesti in the immediate Ploesti area with 20 AAA batteries, four searchlight batteries, and a barrage balloon battalion. The 9th AAA Regiment was deployed with Flakgruppe Vorfeldschutz to the northwest of Ploesti in Prahova valley

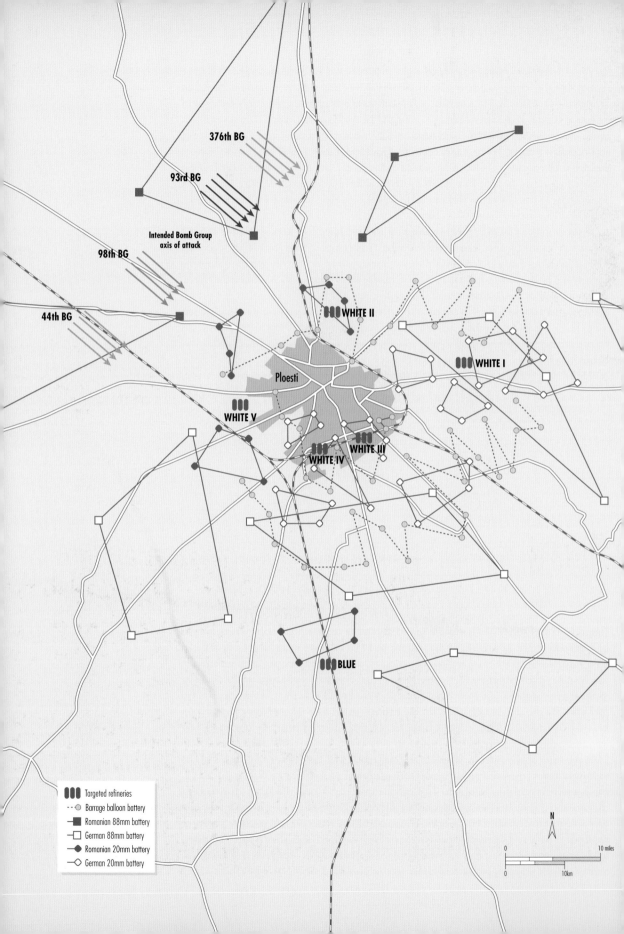

376th BG

93rd BG

Intended Bomb Group
axis of attack

98th BG

44th BG

WHITE II

WHITE I

Ploesti

WHITE V

WHITE III

WHITE IV

BLUE

N

Targeted refineries
Barrage balloon battery
Romanian 88mm battery
German 88mm battery
Romanian 20mm battery
German 20mm battery

0   10 miles

0   10km

including Floreşti (two 20mm batteries), Băicoi-Ţintea (two 88mm batteries, two 20mm batteries), Câmpina (four 88mm batteries, two 20mm batteries), and Moreni (one 20mm battery) with a total of 14 AAA batteries and two searchlight batteries.

German Flak defense

In October 1940, the Luftwaffe began to deploy a special mission to Romania for the defense of the Prahova Valley/Ploesti and other key sites. Generalmajor Wilhelm Spiedel served as the Kommandierender General und Befehlshaber der Deutschen Luftwaffe in Rumänien, with his headquarters in the Lupeshtsi suburb of Bucharest. The initial force consisted of Luftwaffe Flak regiments, searchlight units, and Luftwaffe fighter units.

The first significant Luftwaffe Flak unit deployed for the defense of Ploesti in late 1940 was a Flak Lehr Regiment, subsequently renamed as Flak-Regiment.180. This regiment would form the core of the Ploesti air defenses through 1944. By early 1941, it included 16 88mm batteries, seven 20mm batteries, and one 37mm battery.

One of the first efforts by Luftwaffe air defense specialists was the creation of a full-scale decoy, mimicking the appearance of Ploesti at night. This was intended to lure away night bomber attacks. The first of these was created between Komĕřu and Albesti, 18 miles (30km) southeast of Ploesti. The site was roughly similar in size and layout to Ploesti with false

Besides the large number of 20mm and 88mm Flak, the Ploesti defenses included numerous machine guns such as this Romanian twin 7.9mm water-cooled machine gun.

streets and mock-up structures of wood and canvas. The decoy site included a network of street lights to create an appropriate appearance at night. The mock refineries included burn pits, filled with crude oil, that could be remotely ignited to simulate damage. A number of antiaircraft searchlights were deployed around the fake city. When enemy aircraft appeared within 75 miles (120km) of Ploesti, orders were issued to turn off the actual city lights and to turn on the false street lights. When the enemy aircraft were within 37 miles (60km), the searchlights at the dummy site were turned on.

This decoy system was effective against the initial Soviet night raids. It was useless on the July 13, 1941 daylight raid that approached the city from the northeast instead of the usual approach across the Black Sea from the southeast. By late July 1941, the Luftwaffe presumed that the Soviet units had become aware of the decoy city. A second Ploesti decoy was created west of Cioran, about 19 miles (30km) southeast of the Ploesti Decoy No. 1. When Soviet attacks resumed in August, the lights in Ploesti Decoy No. 2 were turned on. The Soviet pilots assumed this was the dummy city and continued toward Ploesti. In the meantime, the lights in Ploesti Decoy No. 1 had been turned on, and the Soviet aircraft bombers attacked this decoy. This ruse lasted until August 18, by which time the Soviet Black Sea Fleet had determined that a second false city had been created. Soviet aircraft avoided the decoys and attacked the real targets. As a result, the Luftwaffe created Ploesti Decoy No. 3 near Brateshanka, 4 miles (7km) west of Ploesti. The three dummy cities managed to confuse the Soviet pilots and to substantially reduce the damage caused by the summer 1941 Soviet air raids. The Soviet attacks petered out after August 1941 due to the advance of the German and Romanian armies along the Black Sea coast and the loss of critical air bases on Crimea in the fall of 1941.

In anticipation of the invasion of the Soviet Union and possible Soviet air attacks, the Flak defenses in the Ploesti area were expanded in the spring of 1941 to divisional size under the direction of Luftverteidigungskommando.10 (Air Defense Command 10), led

Luftwaffe Flak units began moving into Romania in the fall of 1941 to help defend key Romanian facilities including Ploesti. This is a 40mm Flak 28 position near Giurgiu, Romania on February 28, 1941 covering a key military bridge over the Danube on the Romanian-Bulgarian frontier.

by Generalleutnant Johann Siefert. It followed the usual Luftwaffe Flak organization with two regional formations, Flakgruppe Ploesti and Flakgruppe Vorfeldschutz (Perimeter defense), sometimes called Flakgruppe Băicoi. These were reinforced regiments consisting of a Flak-Regiment with associated support units such as searchlights. Flakgruppe Ploesti was responsible for the defenses in the immediate vicinity of Ploesti while Flakgruppe Vorfeldschutz covered the northwest approaches to Ploesti in Prahova valley, mainly in the area of Băicoi and Câmpina. In turn, each group was divided into Untergruppen with one or more Flak battalions (Abteilungen). These battalions typically included five Flak batteries. The usual pattern was to place the heavy batteries, armed mainly with 88mm guns, furthest from the city, followed by another belt of light batteries, armed with 20mm and 37mm Flak guns, for close range defense.

A searchlight battalion (Scheinwerfer) unit was assigned to Ploesti with three batteries in Flakgruppe Ploesti and the remaining battery with Flakgruppe Vorfeldschutz. The organization of the force at the time of the outbreak of the war in the summer of 1941 is depicted in the chart below.

A Luftwaffe 20mm Flak 30 automatic cannon stationed in a tank farm near Ploesti. These weapons were the most destructive element of Luftwaffe and Romanian defenses during *Tidal Wave*.

Flakgruppe Ploesti	HQ, Flak-Regiment.180
Untergruppe Ploesti-Ost	Res. Flakabt.904, Res.Flakabt.191
Untergruppe Ploesti-Sud	Res. Flakabt.183
Untergruppe Ploesti-West	Res. Flakabt.507
Untergruppe Scheinwerfer	Res. Flakscheinw.Abt. 909
Flakgruppe Vorfeldschutz (Băicoi)	HQ, Flak-Regiment.229
Untergruppe Vorfeldschutz Ost	Res. Flakabt.147
Untergruppe Vorfeldschutz Süd	Res. Flakabt.761

The Luftwaffe Flak battalions were deployed in greatest concentration towards the east and southeast of Ploesti. This was the corridor from the Black Sea that was used most heavily by attacking Soviet bombers in the summer of 1941. The Romanian batteries were positioned mainly to the west and northwest of Ploesti.

On September 1, 1941, Luftverteidigungskommando 10 was redesignated as the 10.Flak-Division. There was considerable pressure to shift inactive Flak units to the battlefront due to critical shortages in Russia. As the threat of Soviet air attack against Ploesti abated in early 1942, the Luftwaffe succumbed to the temptation to shift more responsibility for the Ploesti Flak defense to the Romanians. Some of the Ploesti gun batteries and other equipment was transferred to Romanian control starting in January 1942, as mentioned above. In May 1942, the 10.Flak-Division was detached to Heeresgruppe Süd, though Flak-Regiment.180 remained in the Ploesti area.

The June 12, 1942 raid by the dozen HALPRO B-24D Liberators did little damage to Ploesti but provoked "a panic" in Bucharest and Berlin, according to Romanian accounts. The Luftwaffe began a major reorganization and reinforcement of air defenses around Ploesti. Generalmajor Alfred Gerstenberg, who had served as the air attaché at the embassy in Bucharest since February 1942, was reassigned as the Befehlshaber der Deutschen Luftwaffe in Rumänien in place of Gen Spiedel. Gerstenberg saw the HALPRO raid as merely the forerunner for expanded bomber attacks. Gerstenberg had served as a pilot in the Great War with Luftwaffe chief Hermann Göring, and he had considerable political influence in Berlin as a result. He convinced the governments both in Berlin and Bucharest that Allied air attacks against Romania were likely to accelerate in 1943 and that much more elaborate defenses would be required to survive the onslaught. This included not only additional antiaircraft gun and fighter units, but

In 1942, the Luftwaffe began to deploy many of its heavier 105mm and 128mm Flak guns to railway carriages to permit them to be moved between objectives. This was one of the 128mm Flak 40 auf Geschützwagen schwere Flak Eisenbahnlafette deployed in a protected siding near Boldești-Scăeni, 9 miles (15km) north of Ploesti and seen here in the fall of 1944.

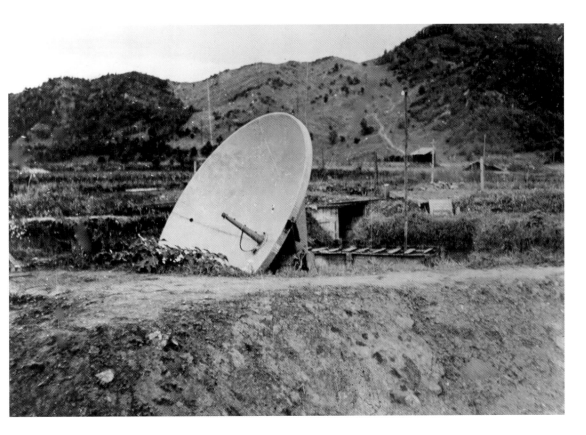

an integrated air defense network with modern radars. In addition, passive defenses were substantially improved including fortification of the Romanian refineries with blast walls to minimize bomb damage, modernization of the fire fighting forces in the refineries, and the creation of a pipeline around the city to link the various refineries. Gerstenberg also recommended that the defense of Festung (Fortress) Ploesti be unified under Luftwaffe control.

Marshal Ion Antonescu visited Hitler's forward command post, Führerhauptquartier Werwolf near Vinnitsa in Ukraine on September 23, 1942. In the wake of the HALPRO raid, he urged the Germans to take stronger measures regarding the defenses of the Ploesti/Prahova valley refineries. Over the next few months, a political and economic protocol was prepared, finally signed on June 17, 1943, that led to a significant German commitment to the defense of the Ploesti/Prahova valley oil region in return for fuel concessions from Romania. Part of the agreement was that Romania would cede control of the defense effort to the Luftwaffe.

As a result of these discussions, Hitler agreed to halt the reduction of Luftwaffe Flak units in Romania and to begin their expansion. The 5.Flak-Division under Generalmajor Julius Kuderna was assigned to the Ploesti mission in December 1942. It retained a deployment pattern of the previous 10.Flak-Division based around Flak-Regiment.180 and Flak-Regiment.202. The heavy Flak batteries were gradually modernized in 1942–43 with Würzburg fire control radars. These were used to direct the searchlights at night. As more radars were added, they were directly attached to the heavy gun battalions for fire direction. By the beginning of 1943, there were nine Würzburg radar stations in the vicinity of Ploesti. A further six stations were added during the summer of 1943 as part of the modernization of defenses.

To further reinforce the Flak defenses, heavy 105mm and 128mm Flak batteries, mounted on railcars for mobility, were assigned to the area. The Flak trains (Eisenbahn Flak) were

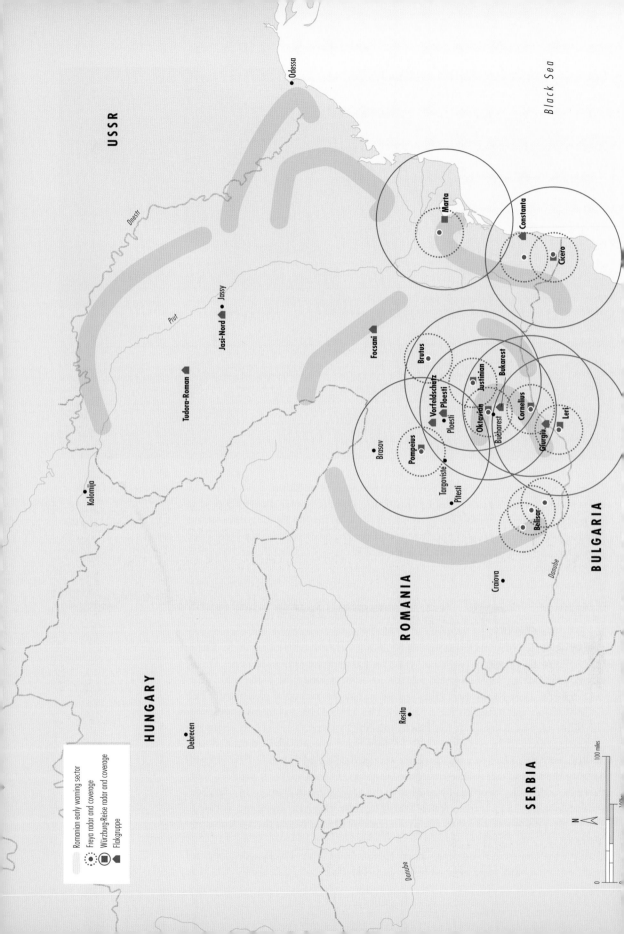

Black Sea

USSR

HUNGARY

SERBIA

ROMANIA

BULGARIA

Odessa

Dnestr

Prut

Jassy

Jasi-Nord

Tudora-Roman

Kolomija

Debrecen

Resita

Craiova

Danube

Danube

Marta

Constanta

Cicero

Focsani

Brutus

Bukarest

Justinian

Vorfeldschutz

Ploesti

Oktavian

Bucharest

Cornelius

Leri

Giurgiu

Brasov

Pompeius

Targoviste

Pitesti

Belisar

Romanian early warning sector

Freya radar and coverage

Würzburg-Reise radar and coverage

Flakgruppe

N

0   100 miles
          100 km

based at the Crângul Lui Bot railroad station in the Prahova valley and Buda to the northeast of Ploesti.

One of the minor mysteries of the Ploesti defenses was the presence of a Flak train operating along the Câmpina-Ploesti railway line at the time of the *Tidal Wave* attack. As will be described later, the Flak train engaged the incoming 98th and 44th Bomb Groups. It was called the "Q-Train" in some American accounts, named after German "Q-Ships." The bombers' crews claimed that the train consisted of Flak guns disguised behind false sides, which lowered when going into combat. This actually sounds like normal German Eisenbahn Flak railway cars, which usually had folding sides that were used to give the gun crews a larger work area when operating the guns from stationary positions. However, German Eisenbahn Flak was not designed to operate while on the move. It would be nearly impossible to operate the heavy Flak from a moving train. The American descriptions seem more compatible with a leichte Eisenbahn-Transportschutz-Flak-Abteilung (Light Railway Transport Protection Flak unit) that were used for railway security and generally armed with light Flak cannon. None are known to have been deployed in Ploesti, though it is certainly possible that one was transiting through the area that day. It is also possible that 5.Flak-Division made an improvised light Flak train using available resources. Romanian accounts do mention the German use of 20mm and 13mm automatic cannon on the railways in the Ploesti area. Some accounts refer to this train as "Die Raupe" (The Caterpillar) and indicate that it was commanded by Hauptmann Joseph Brem. Detailed German accounts are lacking.

Romania's principal indigenous fighter was the IAR 80. These particular aircraft are the IAR 81 variant, designed as fighter-bombers. These were later used in the fighter role and seen here with Escadrila 59 Vt. of the 6 Grupul which took part in the defense of Ploesti in August 1943.

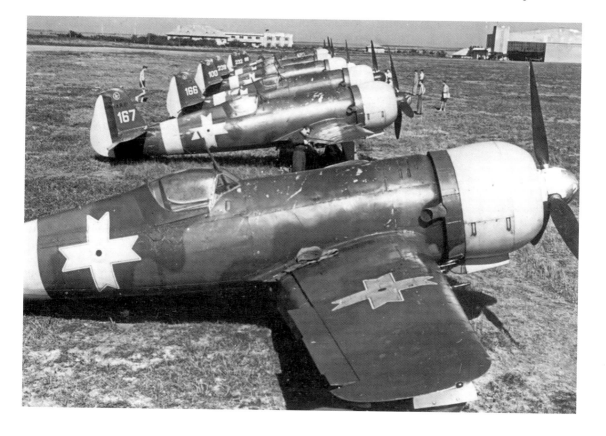

Marshall Ion Antonescu and air force chief Ermil Gheorghiu attend an awards ceremony for Romanian fighter pilots on July 2, 1943. These pilots were veterans of the air campaigns on the Russian Front.

German/Romanian passive defenses in the Ploesti area included static balloons and smoke generators. The Luftwaffe had deployed the Luftsperr-Ballone-Abt.102 to Romania as part of the air defense effort. The standard German barrage balloon was hydrogen-inflated with a capacity of $7{,}065\text{ft}^3$ (200m^3), and was usually flown at an altitude of 6,000–8,000ft (1,800–2,500m). The balloon trailed a steel cable intended to damage or destroy an intruding aircraft. In October 1942, the Luftwaffe turned over responsibility for the barrage balloon barrier to the Romanian 3rd Balloon Battalion (Divizionul 3 Aerostatje). The balloon equipment was deployed in three balloon barriers, one line north of the city, and a double line south of the city. A total of 58 balloons were on hand, but actual operational strength varied. For example, in late July 1943 there were only 18–28 balloons available due to equipment problems, shortage of hydrogen, and a lack of trained crews. On August 1, 1943, a total of 41 balloons were operational.

There was also a static smoke generator battalion with four batteries equipped with a thousand Nebeltopf remotely activated smoke generators to obscure the oil refineries during daylight attacks. These smoke generators were extremely unpopular with the Flak troops since the chemically generated smoke was a serious eye irritant and the smoke obscured the optical fire controls of the Flak batteries.

At the time of the Operation *Tidal Wave* attack in August 1943, the Ploesti/Prahova valley defenses included 36 heavy Flak batteries with 164 88mm and 105mm guns and 16 light batteries with 210 20mm and 37mm automatic cannon. Of these, the 5.Flak-Division had 42 batteries including five 20mm or 37mm light batteries, 32 88mm heavy batteries, and five 105mm/128mm heavy batteries. It was sometimes claimed that these were the strongest air defenses in Europe, though the Flak commands in Berlin and the Ruhr would have disagreed.

Antiaircraft Artillery in the Ploesti Area, August 1943	
5.Flak-Division	Generalmajor Julius Kuderna
Flakgruppe Ploesti	
Flak-Regiment.180	Oberst Oskar Bauer
Regimentul 7 Artilerie Antiaeriană	Colonel Gheorghe Turtureanu
Flakgruppe Vorfeldschutz	
Flak-Regiment.202	Oberst Wilhelm Zabel
Regimentul 9 Artilerie Antiaeriană	Colonel Marius Popeea

Ploesti's fighter defenses

Fighter defenses in the Prahova valley/Bucharest area included elements of the FARR (Forţele Aeriene Regale Române – Royal Romanian Air Force) and the Luftwaffe. In general, the Romanian fighter units were assigned the air sector west of Ploesti/Bucharest while the Luftwaffe was assigned the sector to the east.

The FARR deployed four day-fighter squadrons and one night-fighter squadron in the vicinity of Ploesti. Escadrila 45 Vânătoare (45th Fighter Squadron) was part of Grupul 4 while Esc. 61 and Esc. 62 were part of Grupul 6. Two Romanian squadrons were equipped with newer German fighters, the Bf 109G-2 and Bf 110 night fighter, and were based alongside the German squadrons. So they were alternately referred to by German squadron designations. The German pilots were dismissive of the new Romanian Bf 109G squadron and one remarked that: "Most of the Romanian pilots were wealthy boys from the sporty set. They took poor care of their aircraft. Considering how little they flew, they wrecked many Messerschmitts. But every time they got a new one, a bearded Orthodox priest would visit and bless it." The Germans nicknamed the Romanians flying the smaller IAR 80 fighters as "the Gypsies" and they were regarded as aggressive and daring pilots.

The IAR 80 was an indigenous Romanian fighter that had evolved out of the imported Polish PZL P.24 fighter. It was a low-wing monoplane with a radial engine. A portion of the production had been built in the IAR 81 configuration as a light fighter-bomber. Some of these were modified in 1942–43 by omitting the bomb racks and equipping them with cannon to serve as day-fighters. The text here refers to all versions of this fighter as the IAR 80, though it should be kept in mind that a range of variants took part in the Ploesti fighting.

The Luftwaffe began deploying fighter units to Romania at the beginning of 1941, starting with III./Jagdgeschwader.52 under Maj Gotthard Handrick. The Luftwaffe

A ground crew assists Lt. Mircea Dumitrescu, a pilot of Escadrila 61, Grupul 6 into the cockpit of his IAR 81C.

fighter force near Ploesti was originally called the Ölschutzstaffel (Oil Defense Squadron). These units saw considerable fighting in the summer of 1941 during the Soviet air offensive against Romania, but after the fall of 1941, it was a quiet sector. Various units rotated through the Ploesti area through 1941–43, some to recuperate and rebuild after the fighting in neighboring Ukraine. By the summer of 1943, the force near Ploesti had been expanded to three day-fighter and two night-fighter squadrons. The most common day-fighter was the Messerschmitt Bf 109G-2, though there were small numbers of the newer Bf 109G-6 in service. The night fighters were primarily Bf 110E and 110F. Gerstenberg believed that the most likely Allied bombing attack on Ploesti would be an RAF night attack, and so he went to considerable pains to build up a night-fighter force. The IV./NJG.4 deployed to Ploesti in the summer of 1943, and was led by a Knight's Cross night-fighter pilot, Hermann Lütje.

Romanian records indicate that there were 108 fighter aircraft (56 Romanian, 51 German) in the Ploesti-Bucharest area on August 1, 1943. Since it was Sunday, a significant number of pilots and aircrew were away from base at the time of the American raid. As a result, only 57 aircraft (31 Romanian, 26 German) took part in intercepting the American bombers.

The pilot of an IAR 80 or IAR 81 waits in the cockpit of his aircraft for the take-off order. The FARR units in the Ploesti area waited on the runway for about three hours on August 1 after having received early warnings from Luftwaffe air defense networks in Serbia and Bulgaria.

Fighter Squadrons in Ploesti Area, August 1943		
Unit	**Aircraft**	**Base**
FARR		
Escadrila 45 Vânătoare	IAR 80	Târgşorul Nou
Escadrila 51 Vt. de noapte (12./NJG.6)	Bf 110C	Zilişţea
Escadrila 53 Vt. (4./JG.4)	Bf 109G	Mizil
Escadrila 61 Vânătoare	IAR 80	Pipera
Escadrila 62 Vânătoare	IAR 80	Pipera
Luftwaffe		
I/Jagdgeschwader.4	Bf 109G	Mizil
10./Nachtjagdgeschwader.6	Bf 110E/F	Zilişţea
11/Nachtjagdgeschwader.6	Bf 110E/F	Zilişţea

The Imperator air defense network

Luftwaffe forces in Romania were part of a larger network in southeast Europe, and linked together with neighboring commands in Serbia, Bulgaria, and Greece. One of the most valuable aspects of this network was to provide the various headquarters with early warning of Allied air missions in the region. The Luftwaffe's Chi-Stelle signals intelligence service monitored Allied air force radio transmissions via a network of radio intercept stations. The stations around the eastern Mediterranean reported to the regional W-Leit Südost command post at Megara near Athens. The station on Crete was primarily responsible for monitoring Allied air force radio channels in North Africa, and had been assigned the task of monitoring the USAAF IX Bomber Command in Libya.

While it has often been claimed that the Luftwaffe knew about the *Tidal Wave* mission due to decryption of Ninth Air Force radio signals, German accounts suggest that the first warnings of the *Tidal Wave* mission came from simple radio traffic analysis at W-Leit Südost. In the event, information from the W-Leit Südost station served as early warning to alert the network of radar and observer posts around the Mediterranean and the Balkans when an attack was suspected. Radars of this era had a poor mean-rate-between-failures due to the lack of durability of many of their electronic components. So they were not kept operating on a 24-hour, 7-days-a-week basis. As a result, the radars were only activated when needed. Traditional methods of air early warning were retained including observer posts and some acoustic listening posts.

Beyond the coastal radars, the Luftwaffe had gradually expanded its network of long-range search radars in the Balkans through 1943 on the expectation of Allied bombing missions from North Africa and Sicily. This included stations in Serbia and Bulgaria on the path of the *Tidal Wave* mission to Ploesti. Information from these stations was passed on to the relevant fighter control centers.

After the June 1942 HALPRO raid, the Luftwaffe began to establish an integrated air defense network in the Balkans which provided early warning of impending bomber attack, monitored Allied bomber missions in the Balkans, and provided radar-directed ground-control intercept (GCI) for the fighter force and radar direction for the heavy Flak batteries. This was patterned on the Kammhuber Line in Germany and the Low Countries, though on a much smaller scale. The Romanian network was codenamed Imperator (Emperor), and the radar stations were given Roman names of emperors and historical figures.

The German early warning network in Romania in 1943 consisted of long-range Freya radars with two stationed on the Black Sea coast and a second belt located inland, but also oriented toward potential threats from the Black Sea. Coverage to the north and west was less developed, a gap that would be exploited by the Operation *Tidal Wave* plan. It is unclear whether Allied intelligence knew of the radar gap to the northwest, or whether it was coincidence that the *Tidal Wave* route approached via this radar gap.

By the summer of 1943, the Luftwaffe established Jagdfliegerführer (Jäfu) fighter control stations throughout the Balkans. These regional fighter control stations paralleled the Jagddivision (fighter division) command posts used for the defense of the Reich. These stations were able to take advantage of advances in fighter interception technology that emerged in 1943.

Jäfu Rumänien was headquartered at Otopeni air base in the northern suburbs of Bucharest and subordinated to Luftflotte 4. In the immediate area, Jäfu Rumänien was

One form of passive defense used at Ploesti was the dispersal of hundreds of chemical smoke generators around the city to create artificial fog. However, the smoke proved a hindrance to the Flak crews and was not dense enough to obscure the refineries.

The Telefunken FuMG.65 Würzburg-Riese (Giant Wurzburg) radar deployed at Jägerleit Stellung Oktavian located in Săftica. This type of radar was primarily used for ground-control intercept functions as part of the Jäfu Rumänien fighter control network and there were two of these at this site.

supported by two radar stations, Oktavian near Otopeni, and Pompeius, north of Ploesti. These stations had long-range Freya search radars for early warning and Würzburg-Reise radars as height-finders. The I./Nachtrichtung-Regiment.250 in the Ploesti/Bucharest area was responsible for the radar network in the area as well as other elements of the fighter control system. Both day fighters and night fighters were fitted with a transponder that was part of the Y-Führung (Wotan II/Benito) system, a type of radio direction/range system, linked with search radars. This was later followed by the Jägerleit EGON system in 1944. Data from the early warning network was fed to the Jäfu Gefechtstand (battle station) at Otopeni. This data was plotted on a situation map to serve as the basis for a ground-controlled interception process.

Jäfu Rumänien was commanded by Oberstleutnant Bernhard Woldenga but he was on leave on August 1, 1943. As a result, the command center was headed that day by his Ia (chief of operations) Oberstleutnant Douglas Pitcairn von Perthshire. The day-fighter staff was headed by Major Hermann Schultz and the night-fighter staff by Major Werner Zahn. Jäfu Rumänien also controlled the Romanian squadrons via the Romanian fighter control station codenamed Tigrul (Tiger) based at Pipera. Jäfu Rumänien was linked to other Luftwaffe fighter control and radar centers in the region including Jäfu Balkan in Belgrade, Serbia and Jäfu Bulgarien in Sofia.

The Romanian air force had an existing network of passive early warning sites. These consisted primarily of observer posts reinforced by a small number of acoustic listening posts. The two main belts faced the Black Sea and Hungary. In 1942, the Luftwaffe began modernizing this force by providing radio monitoring stations. The first Romanian units modernized in this fashion were Bateria 286 de pândă radio, stationed in southwestern Romania, and Bateria 282 on the lower Danube. These often proved useful in providing early warning of advancing enemy aircraft, and were linked to the Luftwaffe's W-Leit Südest signals intelligence network.

The Bulgarian fighter force

The Bulgarski voennovozdushni sili (BVS: Bulgarian Air Force) engaged *Tidal Wave* both on the inbound and outbound portions of the mission, since the bombers flew over Bulgaria for a portion of the flight. Jäfu Bulgarien in Sofia coordinated the BVS with the Luftwaffe radar and early warning network in the Balkans. The Bulgarian fighters were deployed with the 6th Fighter Regiment (6 iztrebitelen polk) headquartered at Karlovo and divided into three wings (orlyaki) which were in turn each divided into three squadrons (yati). Two of the wings were equipped with the obsolete Czechoslovak Avia B.534 "Dogan" biplane fighter while the third was converting to the new Bf 109G-2 "Strela." The B.534 were not equipped with an oxygen system, and so their maximum flight altitude was limited.

Unit	Squadrons (yati)	Type	Base
6 iztrebitelen polk	–	–	Karlovo
1/6 iztrebitelen orlyak	612, 622, 632	B.534	Bozhurishche
2/6 iztrebitelen orlyak	642, 652, 662	B.534	Vrazhdebna
3/6 iztrebitelen orlyak	672, 682, 692	Bf 109G	Karlovo

A view of Jägerleit Stellung Oktavian located in Săftica, immediately north of the Oktavian fighter control bunker at the Otopeni air field where Jäfu Rumänien was based. The FuMG.65 Würzburg-Riese air surveillance radar to the left was one of two at the site and was used to locate and track enemy aircraft; the main antenna is folded down in this photo. The Freya-EGON to the right was part of the ground-control interception system, keeping track of friendly fighters via its transponder system. This system was added in 1944.

CAMPAIGN OBJECTIVES
Crippling the refineries

Chief planner for *Tidal Wave* was Col Jacob Smart, seen here on the left, who served on the Air Corps Advisory Council and staff of General "Hap" Arnold, Chief of Staff of the Army Air Force, seen here on the right.

At the start of the German invasion of the Soviet Union in June 1941, the Ploesti area possessed about 85 percent of Romania's refining capacity, about 8.8 million metric tons annually of the country's 10.7 million capacity. Not all this capacity was used, due to limited supplies of crude oil. There was an annual production of about 4.3 million metric tons of refined fuels coming from the Ploesti refineries out of a national total of 4.8 million metric tons.

The major Ploesti refineries			
	Target codename	**Processing capacity (metric tons)**	**Crude oil processed Jan–Jun, 1941**
Astra Română	White IV	2,000,000	567,065
Concordia Vega	White II	1,470,000	341,698
Română Americana	White I	1,400,000	333,676
Steaua Română (Câmpina)	Red	1,240,000	203,930
Unirea Orion	White IV	720,000	184,299
Colombia Aquila	White V	540,000	140,254
Creditul Minier (Brazi)	Blue	540,000	164,650
Petrol Block Standard	White III	504,000	208,298
Unirea Speranța	White III	441,000	52,852
Total		**8,855,000**	**2,196,722**

Although the 1940 British plans to interdict Germany's oil supplies from Romania never had any results, they provided an important resource in the form of a large amount of data collected by the British armed forces for any possible mission. Allied information on the Ploesti refineries was extremely detailed since many of the refineries had been owned by British, French, or American firms before the war. Indeed, the *Tidal Wave* planning committee included at least one officer who had been a refinery manager at Ploesti before the war.

In January 1942, Col Bonner Fellers, the US military attaché in Cairo, suggested attacks on Ploesti as a significant strategic opportunity. There were no US heavy bomber units in the Middle East at the time. The US War Plans Division acknowledged that a B-24 mission could reach Ploesti from Britain, but that the penetration of German defenses along such a long route would result in prohibitive casualties. American interest in Romanian oil was amplified by the Royal Air Force; Air Chief Marshal Arthur Tedder offered British support in April 1942 for any bombing mission. It was largely this early discussion about Ploesti in Washington and Egypt that triggered the impromptu HALPRO raid in June 1942. The issue was also raised with the Soviet government with an idea to stage a shuttle raid, with US bombers landing in the Soviet Union after the Ploesti mission, and then attacking again during the return flight. Moscow ignored the initial inquiries.

A revival of interest in attacking Ploesti took place in 1943 after the American heavy bomber force in Europe expanded. Lt Col C. V. Whitney, assistant air intelligence officer of the Ninth Air Force, submitted a plan called "Project R" to Maj Gen Lewis Brereton, Ninth Air Force commander, in January 1943. Due to the limited resources available at the time to Ninth Air Force, Project R envisioned a mission by 48 bombers departing from Aleppo in northern Syria, transiting over neutral Turkey, and attacking six refineries near Ploesti. The plan was shelved due to a lack of resources, but it was dusted off again when Whitney was transferred back to Washington. A more ambitious plan was outlined

This highly detailed 1:50,000 scale model of Ploesti was prepared by the Central Interpretation Unit at RAF Medmenham for *Tidal Wave* training. It shows the five targeted refineries in the immediate vicinity of the city: 1 (White I: 376th Group), 2 (White II: 93rd Group); 3 (White III: 93rd Group); 4 (White IV: 98th Group); and 5 (White V: 44th Group).

KEY

✈ Airfield

◎ Location of radar station

USAAF Units ●
1. Tidal Wave attack force

MONTENEGRO

4

3

2

ALBANIA

14

15

1

GREECE

Athens

ade

ROMANIA

BULGARIA

5
6
7
IP 1
8
IP 2
9
IP 3
Ploesti
10
Bucharest
11
13
12

EVENTS

1. Around 0822hrs, Flavelle's "Wongo-Wongo" loses control and crashes in the Ionian Sea. At this point, the formations were climbing from their approach altitude of 2,000–3,000ft to about 10,000ft to clear the mountains on the Albanian coast.

2. The formations begin to turn towards the Albanian coast at the northern tip of Corfu around 0855. By this stage, the *Tidal Wave* formations have been spotted by German radars and spotters along the Ionian Sea.

3. The formations begin to pass into Albania around 0900–0910 at an altitude of 10,000ft. Cloud cover over the mountains leads to the separation of the 376th and 93rd Groups in the lead, and the trailing 98th, 44th, and 389th Groups.

4. On reaching the Albanian-Bulgarian frontier around 0935, the lead 376th and 98th Groups were about 30 miles left (northwest) of the planned route and a few thousand feet higher than the trailing 98th, 44th, and 389th Groups.

5. Around 1030hrs, Bulgarian B.534 Dogan fighters of the 6th Fighter Regiment approach the trailing 44th and 389th Groups but are unable to make the intercept.

6. Around 1050hrs, the lead 376th and 93rd Groups reach the Danube along the Romanian frontier and gradually begin the descent to an altitude of 200ft. The trailing 98th, 44th, and 389th Groups reach the same vicinity around 1110hrs.

7. The lead 376th and 93rd Groups reach the first IP (Initial Point) at Piteşti around 1135hrs, followed by the trailing groups around 1155hrs. At Piteşti, the 389th Group breaks off to the northeast to attack Câmpina, immediately north of IP3 Floreşti.

8. Compton, commanding the 376th Group in "Teggie Ann," makes a wrong turn at IP2 at Târgovişte, leading the two lead groups towards Bucharest instead of Ploesti.

9 Around 1205, the 98th and 44th Groups make a proper turn at IP3 Floreşti, heading down the railway line towards Ploesti.

10 The 93rd Group recognizes Compton's navigational error and starts to attack Ploesti around 1155. Compton's 376th Group skirts around Ploesti to the east, bombing "targets of opportunity." The 98th and 376th Groups bomb Ploesti starting at 1213hrs. The 389th Group bombs Câmpina starting at 1214hrs.

11 The original plans called for a rendezvous southwest of Ploesti. With so many bombers badly damaged and many limping back slowly due to damaged engines, the units lose all formation integrity and head back as best they can.

12 Some of the damaged aircraft decide to head south to closer airfields, with five landing on Cyprus and eight heading for Turkey of which one crashed in the sea near the coast.

13 The formations are attacked again by the Bulgarian 6th Fighter Regiment, losing four bombers to Bf 109G-2 Strela fighters.

14 Some of the bombers, running short on fuel, decide to head for closer airfields with eight landing on Sicily, and six on Malta.

15 The III./Jagdgeschwader.27, stationed at Kalamaki/Tanagara airbase on the Greek coast, begin attacking the returning bombers around 1530hrs at altitudes from 3,000 to 6,000ft. The last interception takes place over the Mediterranean at 1713hrs.

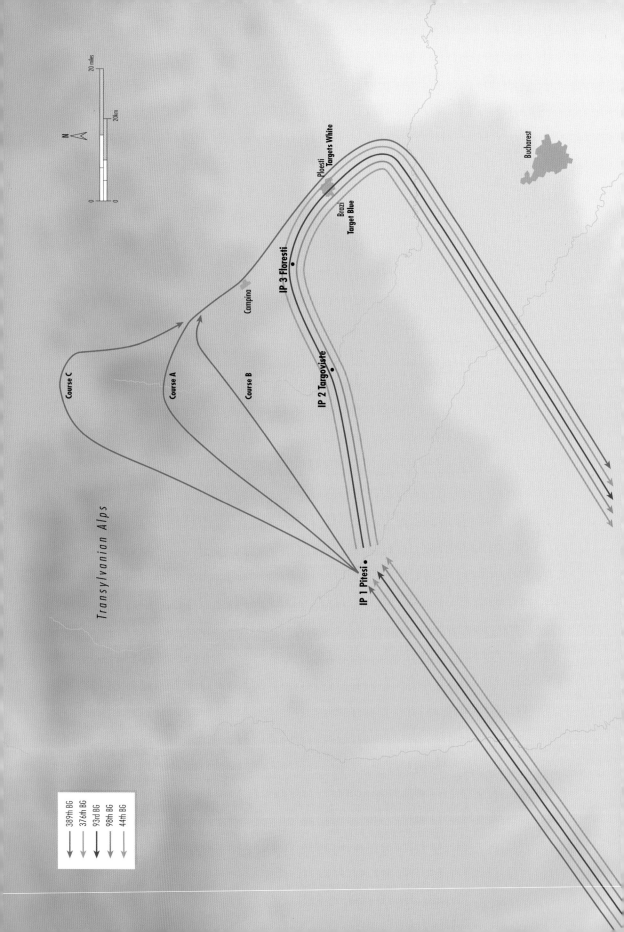

Transylvanian Alps

Course C

Course A

Course B

Campina

IP 3 Floresti

IP 2 Targoviste

IP 1 Pitesi

Ploesti
Targets White

Brazi
Target Blue

Bucharest

N

20 miles
20km
0

389th BG
376th BG
93rd BG
98th BG
44th BG

OPPOSITE *TIDAL WAVE* MISSION: THE PLAN

by Col Jacob Smart in March 1943, proposing a 200-aircraft, low-altitude raid from Benghazi, Libya against nine Ploesti refineries. Smart was on the advisory committee of Chief of the Army Air Forces Lt Gen Henry "Hap" Arnold, and so his proposal received prompter attention in Washington DC. The innovation in the Smart plan was the idea of using B-24 bombers in a low-level mission. Smart acknowledged that such tactics would lead to heavy losses, but he argued that it would be far more effective than the usual high-altitude missions that he estimated would require 2,400 sorties over the course of two months.

Smart convinced Hap Arnold of the value of this plan, which initiated detailed planning. Both the Whitney and Smart plans were presented to the Combined Chiefs of Staff (CCS) on May 13, 1943. This was part of the broader discussions taking place in Washington DC at the Trident Conference between Prime Minister Winston Churchill and President Franklin Roosevelt.

There were some misgivings about the proposal, with Sir Charles Porter, the RAF chief of air staff, wondering whether the diversion of three B-24 squadrons around the time of the Sicily campaign was a prudent use of resources. The US army chief of staff, Gen George Marshall, argued that a successful attack would "stagger the enemy" and would be the best possible aid to the Soviet Union that could be undertaken by US forces in 1943, at a time when the Red Army was bearing the brunt of the ground fighting.

The CCS gave the green light to proceed. The senior Trident leaders, minus Roosevelt, headed to Africa to hold discussions with Gen Dwight Eisenhower, Commander-in-Chief of the North African Theater of Operations (NATO) about Allied strategic planning. Both Eisenhower and his assistant theater commander, RAF Air Marshal Arthur Tedder, approved the Ploesti plan, codenamed Operation *Soapsuds* at this point. Their main reservations were the complications this would cause to Operation *Husky*, the upcoming invasion of Sicily, scheduled for July 1943, since much of the heavy bomber force had been assigned to support this action. Churchill expressed great enthusiasm for *Soapsuds*, except for the name which he felt was not serious enough; it was redesignated as *Tidal Wave*. Churchill offered the services of the four best Lancaster crews with the best navigation experience to lead the mission. Smart demurred, politely mentioning that the performance characteristics of the Lancaster and Liberator were different enough to cause insurmountable problems.

On June 5, 1943, Eisenhower formally approved the *Tidal Wave* mission, recommending that it proceed at the earliest possible date using the two heavy bombardment groups already in NATO, reinforced by three more groups to be transferred from Britain. This was rubber-stamped by the CCS on June 8, 1943. Since one of the strategic objectives of the plan was to assist the Soviet war effort, the issue was raised again about using Soviet bases to permit sustained operations against Ploesti after the initial raid. Moscow largely ignored this idea.

After visiting Britain to obtain RAF technical support, Smart reached the Middle East on July 25 for the first meeting of the *Tidal Wave* Planning Committee. The operation was assigned to Brig Gen Uzal G. Ent's IX Bomber Command. At this time, two major issues were ironed out, high-altitude versus low-altitude attack and Benghazi versus Aleppo as the launch point. Brereton was given final say over the issue. In the event, Benghazi was selected as the launch point since Allied logistical support was far better in Libya than in Syria, even if the distance between Aleppo and Ploesti was shorter.

The issue of low- versus high-altitude attack remained contentious. Aside from arguments about the likely losses to be endured versus accuracy, there was also the issue of the suitability of the B-24D Liberator bomber at low altitude. Col Smart admitted that: "Of all the world's aircraft, there is probably none less suited to ground strafing than the B-24. It is relatively slow…it is clumsy and doesn't react to controls. And to the man on the ground it appears that it can be knocked down with a rock." Smart was not an experienced B-24 pilot, and some of the *Tidal Wave* pilots later criticized his planning of the low-level attack as being unrealistic for so unwieldy an aircraft at low altitudes.

Gen Ent solicited the opinion of the Operations Analysis Section of IX Bomber Command. With the mission objective set as 50 percent destruction of the target set, Ent's team concluded that high-altitude attack would take four missions over nine days. Estimated losses would be 22 bombers of a starting force of about 200 bombers, and the mission would require no special training. On the other hand, Ent concluded that a low-altitude mission might obtain the objectives in a single mission, but that losses might be as high as 75 bombers. Ent recommended high-altitude attack.

Brereton saw the options from a different perspective. The high-altitude plan proposed hitting nine aiming points in each refinery with two 500lb bombs, anticipating further destruction by incidental damage by bombs missing the intended targets, and requiring 2,400 sorties to accomplish the mission. The low-altitude plan was designed to hit 27 aim points with 141 1,000lb bombs, requiring 200 sorties to accomplish the objectives. Brereton decided that *Tidal Wave* would be conducted by a single zero-altitude attack, followed by as many other high- or low-altitude missions as might be required to achieve a desired level of destruction. Lt Harold Korger, bombardier on Kane's B-24D "Hail Columbia" for the Ploesti mission, recalled the disputes among the senior commanders.

Brereton was initially opposed to [Smart's] low-level concept but, once convinced of the plan's merits, he self-admittedly became "caught up in the grandeur of the conception," inviting no discussion whatsoever among his commanders to the point of stressing "the necessity for absolute ruthlessness in the immediate relief of any commander who at any time during the training period showed lack of leadership, of aggressiveness, or of complete confidence." Ent, a well-liked, quiet, pipe-smoking ordained minister, took an instant dislike to Smart's low-level scheme and did not hesitate to voice his objections to his chief, indeed, he openly defied General Brereton's edict of compulsory compliance by encouraging the drawing up of

Tidal Wave bomber allocations							
Target	**Refinery**	**Group Assigned**	**No. of key targets**	**No. of aircraft**	**1,000lb bombs**	**500lb bombs**	**Incendiary bombs**
White I	Română Americana	376th	6	24	24	108	48B*
White II	Concordia Vega	93rd	6	21	48	54	42B
White III	Standard Petrol, Unirea Speranța	93rd	3	12	24	36	24B
White IV	Astra Română, Unirea Orion	98th	10	40	120	60	80B
White V	Colombia Aquila	44th	6	15	36	36	60B
Blue	Creditul Minier (Brazi)	44th	3	18	48	36	36B
Red	Steaua Română (Câmpina)	389th	7	24	48	48	48C
		Reserve		23		92	92C
Totals			**41**	**177**	**348**	**470**	**290B, 140C**
* B= British-type incendiary boxes; C= American-type cluster incendiaries							

a petition opposing the idea among the five group commanders, for which insubordination he very nearly lost his job and career.

With Brereton on board for the low-altitude concept, Col Smart was assigned to develop a more detailed plan. The objective was to render the Ploesti refineries useless for at least four months. As a result, the plan singled out 17 distillation and nine cracking units in the refineries as principal targets. The plan estimated that this could be accomplished by 75 bombers, but to compensate for losses and missed targets, the attack force size was doubled to a minimum of 150 bombers. To further compensate for any losses incurred during support of Operation *Husky*, plus any serviceability issues, the optimum force was set at 200 bombers assigned to the mission.

The premise of the mission planning was that a surprise attack could help minimize losses. As a result, an indirect approach was taken, flying north to Corfu off the Greek coast, with a turn over the sparsely inhabited mountainous regions of Albania and Serbia before turning eastward toward Ploesti. Known German coastal radar sites were avoided, based on secret missions by the B-17 Ferret electronic intelligence aircraft of the 16th Reconnaissance Squadron. At this point, Ferret missions by the USAAF to locate German radars were still in their infancy. The missions in the Mediterranean had only begun in the summer of 1943, and not surprisingly were focused on the Sicily area due to the impending amphibious landings there scheduled for July 1943. A report on German radar installations in the Mediterranean was not available until the eve of the attack. Unbeknownst to the planners or the aircrews, there was a network of German surveillance radars starting on the Greek coast and continuing through the mountains of Serbia and Bulgaria and into Romania.

Detailed knowledge of German antiaircraft defenses in the Ploesti area was poor. There was considerable reluctance to dispatch RAF photo reconnaissance aircraft over Romania for fear that this would alert the Luftwaffe to the forthcoming mission. The presumption was that the area would be heavily defended in view of its strategic importance. Intelligence estimates suggested about 100 medium and heavy AAA guns and "several hundred" light guns; the actual numbers were 164 and 210. Although the numbers were not far off, the intelligence expected the defenses to be heaviest in the north and northwest when in fact they were heaviest in the south and southeast due to the 1941 Soviet attacks and the German presumption that Allied attacks from the Mediterranean would come from the south. The threat to the low-altitude mission was primarily from light 20mm and 37mm batteries since the fire-direction systems of the heavy 88mm batteries were not well suited to engaging fast, low-altitude targets. There was a tendency to deprecate the Flak in the area due to the mistaken belief that the batteries were manned primarily by second-rate Romanian troops.

The Allied intelligence estimated a balloon force of about 100 balloons. This was higher than the actual figure, and it was estimated that a third of all aircraft striking a balloon cable would be lost. From British experience, it was recommended that aircraft would be safer hitting the cable at low altitude, which fitted in to the attack plan.

No German fighters were expected to be encountered in route to Ploesti, though it was presumed that there would be German and Romanian fighters in the Ploesti-Bucharest area. The plan expected that the novel direction and low-altitude of the attack would help dampen the effectiveness of interceptors around Ploesti.

The best date for the attack was expected to be August 1–4. This was the earliest date that would allow sufficient time for training. Furthermore, British intelligence had broken the Luftwaffe weather cipher and so expected clear summer weather for that period. Eventually, August 1 was selected, in large measure since it was a Sunday and there was the presumption that defenses would be distracted and understaffed.

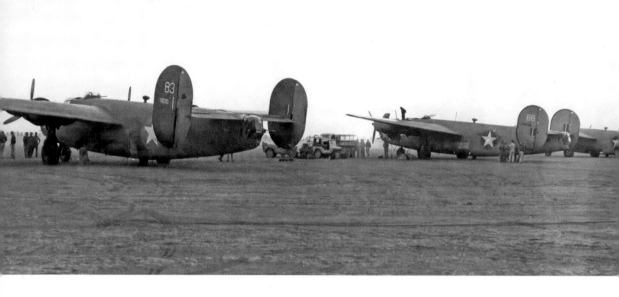

THE CAMPAIGN
A high-stakes raid

Tidal Wave commences

The crews from three of the B-24D bombers of the 515th Squadron, 376th Group man their aircraft in the early morning hours of August 1, 1943. The aircraft from left to right are "Chum-V," "Dopey Goldberg," and "Joey Uptown."

The five bomb groups of the IX Bomber Command began the *Tidal Wave* mission around 0400–0550hrs. A single aircraft from the 98th Group, "Kickapoo," lost an engine shortly after take-off and crashed after attempting to return to base. This left 177 B-24D bombers heading for Romania over the Mediterranean at altitudes of 2,000 to 4,000 feet (600–1,200m).

The lead formation was Col Keith Compton's 376th Group, the Liberandos. Compton's aircraft, "Teggie Ann," included the mission commander, Gen Ent, and the lead navigator, Capt Harold Wicklund, who had flown the previous HALPRO mission to Ploesti. According to the official history of the mission prepared in June 1944, and based on a report by Col Smart: "It was originally planned that Colonel Compton, as commander of the 376th, should lead the formation in the attack. Shortly before taking off, however, he appointed Lt B. W. Flavelle, one of his squadron commanders, leader of the 376th and thus, leader of the whole force."

This change has been the source of considerable controversy as a result of the navigation errors that occurred later in the morning. In the event, Flavelle's leadership of the formation was short-lived. South of Corfu island, Compton ordered the first major change of course and altitude with the formations climbing to 10,000ft to avoid the mountains once they reached the Albanian coast. Around 0820hrs, Flavelle's aircraft "Wongo-Wongo" encountered an unexplained malfunction, made a sharp turn in steep bank and began to fall towards the sea. Attempting to recover around 100 feet, the aircraft crashed into the sea and burned. Flavelle's wingman and close friend, Lt Guy Iovine, piloting "Desert Lilly" broke formation and flew down towards the wreck apparently with an aim towards rendering assistance to any survivors. There were no survivors. Iovine realized he had little chance of joining the formation, and so headed back to base. This left a single aircraft of the lead element, Lt John Palm in "Brewery

Shortly before dawn in the early morning hours of August 1, 1943, the crew of "Doodlebug" of the 512th Squadron, 376th Group is loading .50cal heavy machine gun ammunition in the waist gun position. Outside the aircraft is gunner SSgt Joseph Tamulewicz and inside is radioman TSgt William Jordan.

Wagon," as the nominal lead navigation aircraft. This incident was later described by Col John "Killer" Kane, leading the 98th Group:

> I began a steeper climb to keep from over running the lead (376th) group. We were at 10,000 feet when Johnny (co-pilot Lt John Young) and I were amazed to see the lead plane of the 376th, whoever the leader was, turn end-for-end and spin down into the sea. The plane exploded in a black cloud of smoke. We sat there, stunned, and watched the 376th go to pieces. Planes went in every direction...The leading Group was disorganized and had lost any semblance of a formation.

Ground crew of the 376th Group cleans the plexiglass nose of "Doodlebug" (41-23724) of the 512th Squadron in the early hours of August 1. This aircraft, piloted by Lt John McAtee, survived the *Tidal Wave* mission.

The USAAF history went on to note that:

> Leadership of the formation now devolved upon the deputy leader (Palm), who, without a hitch, proceeded to perform his task, exactly as prescribed. General Ent and Colonel Compton, whose plane was in one of the following elements of the leading group, were not aware of the fact that the plane which had plunged into the sea was that of the leader and of the consequent change in leadership. This change, however, contrary to a notion that has arisen, does not appear to have had any special significance in the subsequent course of events.

The "notion" mentioned in the official account was the allegation that this series of misfortunes was the root cause of the later navigational errors of the 376th Group which so adversely affected the conduct of the *Tidal Wave* mission. In an interview with Robert Sternfels for the revised 2002 edition of his book on the Ploesti raid, Compton offered a very different view of the incident. He categorically stated that he had not relinquished the

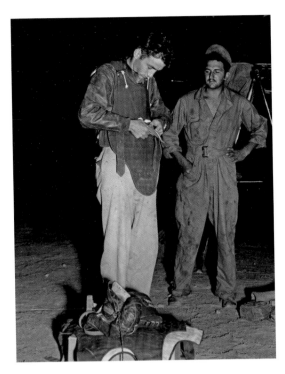

ABOVE LEFT
Lt John McAtee, pilot of "Doodlebug" of the 512th Squadron, 376th Group is seen adjusting his flak apron before boarding his aircraft for the August 1, 1943 *Tidal Wave* mission.

ABOVE RIGHT
In the early morning hours of August 1, 1943, Capt Ralph "Red" Thompson, co-pilot of the command ship "Teggie Ann," helps Brig Gen Uzal Ent fit into a flak apron. To the right is the commander of "Teggie Ann" and commander of the 376th Group, Col K. K. Compton.

lead navigation role to Flavelle, but that his aircraft, "Teggie Ann," with his navigator, Capt Harold Wicklund, remained the mission leader. He also claimed that Flavelle's aircraft was behind "Teggie Ann" when it went down.

An explanation for these discrepancies has not yet emerged. One plausible explanation is that Compton conferred the honor of the "lead navigation" title on Flavelle for his initiative in the April 1, 1943 low-level mission to Messina/Crotone. At the same time, Compton had no intention of relinquishing his role as "Mission Leader." Sternfels, pilot of the B-24D "The Sandman" at Ploesti, later remarked that the controversy was entirely meaningless since there was an ample supply of qualified navigators on the mission and at no time did Flavelle's tragedy have any consequence on the conduct of the mission.

Early detection

In order to ensure surprise, the *Tidal Wave* mission was flown in strict radio silence on the presumption that the Luftwaffe would be intercepting radio signals and use radio direction finding stations to track the flight and determine its destination. In the event, the instructions on radio silence did not prevent the Germans from discovering the mission, and strict adherence to radio silence would have unfortunate consequences later during the mission.

The Luftwaffe Chi-Stelle signals intelligence service had been monitoring USAAF radio traffic in North Africa since 1942. Although the Sicily invasion had forced the evacuation of its stations in July 1943, the W-Leit Südost continued to monitor routine USAAF traffic from its monitoring station on Crete. On the morning of August 1, 1943, the signals intercept station picked up a message from Ninth Air Force headquarters about the departure of a large bomber formation from the Benghazi area. While some American accounts suggest that Luftwaffe cryptologists had broken the Ninth Air Force code, German accounts suggest that the meaning of the message was discerned simply by routine traffic analysis. This information was passed on to the regional Nachrichten.4 headquarters near Athens, and Leutnant Christian Ochsenschlager forwarded this on to "interested parties" including Jäfu Rumänien.

Crews from the 376th Group unload from a 2½-ton truck in the pre-dawn hours of August 1, 1943. The bomber to the left is "Teggie Ann," the mission command ship, and the airmen are probably from its crew.

At Jäfu Rumänien's command post, Oberstleutnant Douglas Pitcairn von Perthshire at first assumed that it was simply another early morning training flight over the Mediterranean. When Luftwaffe radar and observation posts on Corfu spotted the formation over the Ionian Sea around 0800hrs, there was suspicion that it might be heading for the Messerschmitt factory at Wiener Neustadt in Austria, but it might be Ploesti. Pitcairn warned his staff, "All right everyone, let's have a big breakfast. We may be here quite a while." The *Tidal Wave* force reached the Albanian coast near Corfu around 0900hrs, and by this point was flying at an altitude of roughly 10,000ft. The Luftwaffe radar station on Corfu, as well as observers,

B-24D (41-11630) "Chum-V," of the 515th Squadron, 376th Group, piloted by Lt Jerome Dufour, churns up a cloud of dust from its prop wash as it prepares to taxi at Benghazi in the early morning hours of August 1, 1943.

B-24D (42-40664) "Teggie Ann," the *Tidal Wave* command ship piloted by 376th Group commander Col K. K. Compton with the mission commander Brig Uzal Ent on board. It is seen here taxiing shortly before take-off near Benghazi at the start of the mission.

reported the formation and noted that it had made a turn towards Sofia. This information was fed through the Luftwaffe network including Jäfu Rumänien.

Since there was some chance that the bomber formation would attack Ploesti, the fighter squadrons in the Ploesti area were alerted. The Romanian squadrons had the pilots man their fighters in mid-morning, though they remained on the ground for the time being. Jäfu Bulgarien in Sofia was also alerted and this started the process of activating local fighter squadrons and confirming that radar stations and observer posts in the Balkans were on alert.

The loss of formation integrity

The *Tidal Wave* formations encountered heavy cumulus clouds from 10,000 to 15,000ft that became lower as the formations approached Serbia. Since some of the mountains in Serbia towered to 8,000–8,500ft, there was only a narrow layer of about 1,000ft of visibility. There are significant discrepancies in the accounts of how the groups dealt with the unexpected

B-24D (42-40563) "Wongo-Wongo" of the 512th Squadron, 376th Group is seen taking off at dawn on August 1, 1943 at the start of the *Tidal Wave* mission. Piloted by Lt Brian Flavelle, the mysterious and unexplained crash of this aircraft in the Ionian Sea off Corfu has been mistakenly blamed for the navigational problems experienced by Compton's 376th Group later in the mission.

After exiting the cloud-shrouded Dacian Alps in Serbia, the three trailing groups reached clear skies over the Danube basin in western Romania. This view was taken from a B-24D of the 389th Group looking down on aircraft of the 98th and 44th Group below.

weather. The official USAAF history as well as some of the personal accounts indicate that Compton led the 376th Group to an altitude of 16,000ft to clear the clouds, followed by Baker's 93rd Group. Compton later stated that this was a mistake and that he had led the formation through the clouds at 9,000ft. Kane's 98th Group apparently followed a standard USAAF flying technique called "Frontal Penetration," which involves the leader rallying the bombers in a circular flight pattern before entering the clouds as a means to avoid collisions when visibility is lost. Such a maneuver takes time. The two lead formations did not use this technique, but Kane's and the two trailing groups did so. Kane's group, followed by the 44th and 389th Groups, passed through the clouds at 14,000ft.

As a result, as the *Tidal Wave* formation exited the clouds, they had become split between the two front groups led by Compton and the three trailing groups led by Kane. Eventually, Kane's 98th Group regained sight of the advance group, about 30 miles (50km) left of the prescribed course and several thousand feet higher. The instructions about radio silence prevented Kane from contacting Compton, and the lead formation remained uncertain of the location of the three trailing groups.

First interception

In spite of the *Tidal Wave* formation's radio silence, Luftwaffe regional air control had been tracking the bombers intermittently since they had passed the Greek coast. Jäfu Balkan in Belgrade was informed of sightings by the major Luftwaffe radar stations in Serbia. This data was forwarded to Jäfu Bulgarien in Sofia, Bulgaria, which received its own radar sightings around 1000hrs from the Freya radar station on Mount Vitosha near Sofia. The *Tidal Wave* formation crossed from Serbia into Bulgarian air space for a short time. Around 1025hrs, the Bulgarian 6th Fighter Regiment scrambled three of its wings to intercept the intruders. Six Avia B.534 Dogan biplane fighters were scrambled from Vrazhdebna airbase, and four B.534 from Bozhurishche. Ten Bf 109G-2 Strela were sent aloft in two groups, one to provide

Prior to crossing the Danube River on the Bulgarian-Romanian frontier, the Bulgarian 6th Fighter Regiment attempted to intercept the *Tidal Wave* bombers, as shown in this illustration. Although visual contact was made by two Bulgarian Avia B.534 Dogan fighters flown by Lt Vaptsarov and Lt Daskalov, they were too low, too slow, and too short of fuel to complete the interception. The Bulgarian squadrons did attack the bombers on the return flight.

air cover for Sofia and the other to hunt for the bombers. Two B.534 fighters piloted by Lt Vaptsarov and Lt Daskalov sighted the American formation at a distance, but the B-24 bombers were flying too high and too fast for the obsolete fighters to reach them in time. The crews from the trailing 389th Group and 44th Group spotted the Bulgarian fighters and thought they were trying to shadow the formation. Due to the rules about radio silence, Ent and Compton were not informed of this. As a result, the leadership of the *Tidal Wave* mission was unaware that the mission's secrecy was already lost.

The Bulgarian fighters were ordered to return to base for refueling, assuming that they would have a second chance when the bombers returned through Bulgarian airspace later in the day. By this stage, it was fairly evident to Oberstleutnant Pitcairn at Jäfu Rumänien that the target was Ploesti. He ordered his staff to take an early lunch on the assumption that the American formations would begin arriving over the Prahova valley before noon. Fighter squadrons and Flak batteries in the Ploesti area were warned to prepare for action.

The separation of the Compton and Kane formations became worse before reaching the Danube river at the Romanian border around 1100hrs. The leading 376th and 93rd Groups flew over the clouds, enjoying a strong tail wind, while the 98th Group, followed by the 44th and 389th Groups, flew below them at a slower speed. The weather cleared in the vicinity of the Danube. Compton later stated he reduced his speed to 160mph and zig-zagged, hoping the lagging groups would catch up. The tail gunners could not see the trailing groups, and eventually Compton decided to press on into Romania and the objective. The two lead groups were about 15 to 20 minutes ahead of the three trailing groups when they entered Romanian air space. Compton later recalled that "I originally blamed Colonel Kane for not maintaining his position in the formation in accordance with the mission plan." He believed that the loss of group integrity was due to Kane's flying procedure rather than the weather conditions.

As mission leader, Compton could have made the decision to break radio silence in the hopes of re-establishing formation integrity. Compton did not feel that the maintenance of formation integrity was sufficient reason to keep the two lead groups loitering around in enemy airspace while waiting for the arrival of the remaining three groups at some indefinite time in the future. Short radio communication at this time could have clarified the situation but Compton chose radio silence over formation integrity. Strict radio silence compromised command-and-control of the *Tidal Wave* formation and led to a chain reaction of misadventures that undermined the mission.

A disastrous turn

Entering Romania, the first IP (Initial Point) for the *Tidal Wave* force was the town of Piteşti. By this point, Compton's two groups had descended to tree-top level of about 200ft. The navigator onboard "Teggie Ann," Maj Harold Wicklund, prepared an ETA (estimated time of arrival) between the Danube River and the third IP at Floreşti where the groups would make their critical final turn down the Prahova valley to Ploesti. "Red" Thompson, co-pilot of the "Teggie Ann," was flying the aircraft while Compton studied the maps and navigation aids on his lap. On reaching the second IP at Târgovişte, Compton spotted a village with a railroad line heading east. This resembled the depictions of the third IP at Floreşti and, believing that Wicklund's ETA had been reached, Compton ordered Thompson to begin the turn to Ploesti. Compton did not consult Wicklund before giving the order. The turn was premature and sent the two lead groups to the west of Ploesti and towards Bucharest.

Apparently, several pilots and navigators in the 376th Group realized Compton's mistake and attempted to radio him. Compton later stated that he was on the intercom at the time and that the command channel was not being monitored due to the radio silence instructions. The aircraft of the 376th and 93rd Groups, assuming that Compton had decided on a change of direction, followed him to the southeast towards Bucharest.

The remaining three groups, led by Kane's 98th Group, followed about 15–20 minutes after. On reaching the first IP at Piteşti at 1155hrs, the 389th Group separated from the rest of the formation since it was assigned a separate mission against the refineries in the Câmpina area. The 98th Group and 44th Group continued past the second IP at Târgovişte, and began making the final approach to Ploesti after making the turn at the third IP of Floreşti.

Instead of attacking as a single, concentrated force, the *Tidal Wave* formation was now broken up into two groups attacking about 15 minutes apart. While this was later criticized in after-action reports, a significant "what-if?" question remains. If the five groups had remained together after crossing the Danube, would the entire formation have followed Compton and made the wrong turn at Târgovişte? Wouldn't this have undermined the execution of the *Tidal Wave* plan to a far worse extent than what eventually transpired? It is by no means clear that the loss of formation integrity in the passage over Serbia was the most significant factor in undermining the *Tidal Wave* plan. With Compton's two groups wandering astray towards Bucharest, the other three groups were heading to their targets as planned.

Tidal Wave approaches Ploesti

After reaching the third Initial Point at Floreşti, Kane's 98th Group and Johnson's 44th Group made the critical turn towards Ploesti. The 44th Group was on the right and the 98th on the left as seen here, with the Câmpina-Ploesti railway line between them. As they exited the hill country around Floreşti, they began to descend to very low altitude over the flat farm land north of Ploesti. This is a view westward over the middle of Kane's 98th Group with elements of Pike Flight in the foreground. The B-24D bombers of the 98th Group were painted in "Desert Pink," while the 44th Group, having arrived from Britain, were still in the factory "Olive Drab" finish. Both "The Witch" and "Snow White and the Seven Dwarves" survived the bomb run over Ploesti but were shot down by Bulgarian Bf 109G-2 fighters on the return home.

Imperator strikes back

By late morning, the Imperator network in Romania had been warned by Jäfu Bulgarien about the radar tracks into Romania. Romanian spotters in the Transylvanian Alps also saw the formations and reported to Bucharest. The two fighter-control radar stations in the Ploesti vicinity, Pompeius and Oktavian, attempted to track the formation without success. Some Romanian accounts later suggested that the Americans were jamming the radars. However, the early APT-1 Carpet and APT-2 Mandrel jammers were still very new at this stage and there is no evidence that they were fitted to any of the *Tidal Wave* aircraft. The radar problems were due to the low-altitude approach of the *Tidal Wave* groups which were below the radar horizon of the German radar stations due to the hilly conditions in the Prahova valley.

Regardless of the lack of radar tracking, Pitcairn was certain that an attack on Ploesti was imminent. He alerted the headquarters of Flakgruppe Ploesti of the impending arrival of the bombers. Flak-Regiment.180's headquarters in turn contacted its subordinate German and Romanian Flak batteries and ordered them to full alert at 1115hrs. The Romanian 3rd Balloon Battalion struggled to get their huge balloons in the air. Out of the 58 balloons on hand, they managed to get 41 aloft around 1150hrs. The situation with the smoke generation units was less successful. These units had been the first alerted around 1055hrs. However, the units had to be taken out of storage and deployed. Of the thousand devices on hand, only 274 proved to be functional. Activation of the units did not begin until 1140hrs due to the disorganization of the unit. In the event, the wind conditions were not favorable, and the resulting artificial fog contributed nothing to the defense of Ploesti.

The Romanian and German squadrons in the Bucharest/Ploesti area were scrambled for an intercept starting at 1118hrs. The radar tracks in Bulgaria had spotted the aircraft still at high altitude as they had crossed over the Transylvanian Alps, and the presumption was that the Americans would conduct a normal high-altitude attack on Ploesti. As a result, Pitcairn directed the day-fighter squadrons to climb to a cruise altitude of 16,500ft (5,000m).

The Bf 109G squadrons of Jagdgeschwader.4 left Mizil and took up patrols to the north of Ploesti. Esc. 45 Vt. was sent to patrol the Bilciureşti-Conteşti-Butimanu area southeast of Ploesti, Esc. 53 was directed 6 miles (10km) north of Ploesti alongside the German fighters,

A striking image from a film clip taken during the *Tidal Wave* missions, showing how low some of the bombers flew.

The two Small Würzburg gun-laying radars and three Kommandogerät directors were used to control the guns firing at upper right. An approaching B-24D can be seen on the horizon in the upper center, flying through heavy flak.

and the night fighters of Esc. 51 were sent to the Bolintin-Deal area west of Bucharest. The two German night-fighter squadrons were sent aloft around 1200hrs to the Crivina-Peris sector east of Ploesti since, by this stage, Compton's errant 376th Group had been spotted.

When the Romanian and German fighters climbed to 16,500ft, they found no American bombers. There was a layer of overcast around 2,000ft which blocked the view below. Around 1145hrs, observer reports began to come in to Pitcairn's Jäfu Rumanian fighter control station about low-altitude American bombers. Pitcairn immediately sent out radio instructions to the fighters to descend to low altitude. The first reported contact occurred around 1150hrs over Săbăreni in the northwestern suburbs of Bucharest between the IAR 80 fighters of Grupul 6 and Compton's 376th Group. Grupul 6 had difficulty making the interception since they began to make their interception passes around the same time that Compton began to swing back toward Ploesti. The Romanian fighters did strike the trailing 93rd Group. One IAR 80 managed to get in range of of Lt Worthy Long's "Jersey Bounce 2nd," hitting the rear gun turret and killing the gunner, Sgt Lycester Havens, the first US casualty of *Tidal Wave*.

The reports of bombers near Bucharest confused Pitcairn, already dismayed by the appearance of the bombers at low altitude instead of the expected high-altitude route. At first, he tried to respond by sending the night fighters towards Bucharest. As more reports arrived, it became clear that Ploesti was the real target. Pitcairn believed that the approach of the American bombers towards Bucharest was a clever ruse to lure away the German and Romanian fighters.

The decision to attack at low altitude did win tactical surprise for the Ploesti mission. As a result, the Romanian and German fighter squadrons wasted considerable time and fuel climbing to high altitude in the half-hour before the bombers actually reached Ploesti. If Pitcairn had not made this mistake, and instead sent the fighters at low altitude up the Prahova valley, the *Tidal Wave* mission would have had to endure 30 minutes of fighter attacks before reaching their Ploesti targets. In the event, the fighters did not begin to engage the bombers until after the bomb runs had begun.

The Liberandos' wayward odyssey

Compton did not become convinced of his navigational mistake until his aircraft was in sight of the northern suburbs of Bucharest. On the horizon were church steeples, not oil refineries. As detailed below, by this time the 93rd Group had already broken away and was headed back to Ploesti on their own.

Lt John Palm, piloting "Brewery Wagon," was the sole surviving aircraft of Flavelle's doomed element. His aircraft was slightly separated from the rest of the Liberandos. Palm's navigator, Lt William Wright, warned him that Compton had made a wrong turn. Accepting Wright's judgment, Palm decided to break off and attack Ploesti on his own. "Brewery Wagon" flew towards Ploesti through a low-lying rain squall, and after exiting the clouds, the bomber was struck by 20mm Flak in the nose and engines, killing the bombardier and severely wounding Wright and Palm. With one engine knocked out and two others damaged, co-pilot William Love salvoed the bombs and tried to escape the area. "Brewery Wagon" was intercepted by a Bf 109 and brought down near Tătărani on the Bucharest-Ploesti railway line. The crew managed to escape the belly landing except for the bombardier and navigator after the nose compartment was crushed during the impact. It is generally acknowledged that "Brewery Wagon" was the first *Tidal Wave* bomber to fall to enemy action.

This fighter attack is usually attributed to Hauptmann Wilhelm Steinmann from the Stab (headquarters flight) of JG.4. However, Steinmann's first claim of the day was in sector SN1, south of Ploesti, but about 6 miles (10km) from where Palm's aircraft crashed, and his interception was the second of the day, around 1204hrs. The first Luftwaffe claim of the day was by Oberleutnant Hans-Wilhelm Schöpper, also assigned to Stab I./JG 4, but leading 2./JG.4 that day in Bf 109G-2 named "Hecht." He later reported the shoot-down occurring at 1200hrs near Bătești, near Palm's crash site. Furthermore, his description of the interception coincides with other known details of the shoot-down of "Brewery Wagon." The one discrepancy in Schöpper's account compared to Palm's recollections was that Palm thought the German fighter had attacked head on. Both Schöpper and Steinmann described their attacks as coming from the rear. Schöpper recalled:

> I saw a B-24 emerging from the smoke that covered Ploesti. It was flying at only 40 meters (130ft). I attacked from the rear and set his right wing on fire. After firing a long burst, I gained altitude to avoid the machine gun fire. Then I maneuvered myself a little to the side to observe my victim and to determine whether I had to conduct a second pass. Since the outbreak of the fire, the pilot tried to gain altitude but didn't succeed and the bomber crashed and broke up in a field. He had probably dropped his bombs before crashing, otherwise it would have exploded. I think some of the crewmen were able to escape.

Moments later, Schöpper spotted a B-24D trailing smoke after it had been hit by a Bf 110 attack, presumably from the 93rd Group. Although he began to make a pass to finish off the bomber, the fuel warning light went on and he was forced to return to Mizil to refuel. This was a common problem for the JG.4 fighters since they had been orbiting overhead for over a half-hour before intercepting the bombers. Leutnant Philipp Bouquet from 3./JG 4 recalled his initial engagement:

> Unfortunately, we intervened after 40 minutes of flight and could not pursue the fugitives. The entire battle took place between five and 100 meters (15–325ft). After becoming separated from my unit, I found myself in the middle of the enemy formation, surrounded

by enemies. What a sensation! But I was angry and attacked one of the rear aircraft, setting a right engine on fire. The aircraft stalled and gradually lost altitude. Unfortunately I could not follow him because I was fired on from my left and had to move away.

Around 1155hrs, Compton and Ent in the "Teggie Ann" finally realized that they had made the turn too early and now were on the outskirts of Bucharest, not Ploesti. They began to make a turn back northward towards Ploesti. In the confusion of the moment, there does not seem to have been much of a discussion about whether or not to attack their planned targets. By this time, Baker's 93rd Group had already begun its strikes on the southeastern side of Ploesti and the area was full of smoke, streams of tracers, and flak bursts. Rather than run that gantlet, Ent told Compton to skirt around Ploesti on the eastern side. The radio message from command ship "Teggie Ann" announced, "We have missed our bomb run. We have missed our bomb run. Strike targets of opportunity. Strike targets of opportunity."

Many participants later recalled that it was General Ent who made the announcement, but years later Compton claimed that it was his message. In the event, it caused considerable confusion since it was unclear what constituted "targets of opportunity." The bombers followed "Teggie Ann" around the eastern side of Ploesti, avoiding the firestorm engulfing the city. Ignoring his bombardier, Compton salvoed his bombs on some tank cars using the pilot's emergency controls. In the haste and confusion, it wasn't clear if the bombs had been armed and they ripped through the bomb-bay doors that had not been opened. Very few of the Liberandos attacked any refineries and some bombers simply salvoed their bombs over empty fields. There were random attacks on rail yards and other apparent targets. The largest concentration of wayward bombs was in the districts of Argeş and Dolj to the east of Bucharest where Romanian police identified the impacts of about 60 bombs in 11 villages. These may have been jettisoned by the 376th Group after the "targets of opportunity" order was given.

The exception to the random bombing was Lt Norman Appold, piloting "G.I. Ginnie." Determined to strike an important target, Appold spotted the Concordia Vega refinery on the northeast corner of Ploesti, one of the intended targets of the 93rd Group. With four other bombers following him, Appold led the attack into the refinery, dropping their payload into a distillation plant in the refinery. This small attack damaged Batteries No. 4 and No. 5 and reduced production from 58,000 metric tons in July 1943 to only 22,000 metric tons in August. However, repairs returned the plant to capacity in September.

The B-24D on the left, (41-24294) "Brewery Wagon" piloted by Lt John Palm, was the only 376th Group bomber lost over Ploesti after Palm broke away from Compton's formation and attacked the refineries on his own. The aircraft to the right is (41-24258) "Desert Lilly" piloted by Lt Guy Iovine. When Flavelle's "Wongo-Wongo" crashed in the Ionian Sea, Iovine circled the crash site hoping to spot survivors. Isolated from the 376th Group, he elected to return to base.

EVENTS

1. At 1118hrs, the IAR 80 fighters of Esc. 45 Vt based at Târgşorul Nou are scrambled and sent to patrol to the Bilciureşti-Conteşti-Butimanu area southwest of Ploesti at an altitude of 16,000ft.

2. At 1118hrs, the two IAR 80 squadrons of Grupul 6 based at Pipera in the northern Bucharest suburbs are scrambled to patrol the area north of the city at an altitude of 16,000ft.

3. Around 1120hrs, the Bf 109G-2 squadrons of I./JG.4 based in Mizil are scrambled to set up an air patrol to the northwest of Ploesti in over the Prahova valley at an altitude of 16,000ft.

4. Around 1135hrs, the 376th and 93rd Groups arrive over IP1 of Piteşti and continue on to IP2.

5. Around 1145hrs as the 376th and 93rd Groups pass over IP2 at Târgovişte, Col K. K. Compton makes a navigation error and begins prematurely to turn the two groups to the southeast toward Bucharest instead of Ploesti.

6. Col Baker, leader of the 93rd Group, realizes that Ploesti is immediately to the east and turns his group to attack the nearest refineries on the southwest side of Ploesti.

7. Shortly before noon, the German and Romanian fighter squadrons are ordered to descend rapidly and engage the bomber waves around Ploesti. The first interceptions occur southwest of the city.

8. Shortly before noon, Compton sees the cathedral spires of Bucharest ahead. Realizing he has made a navigational error, he turns the 376th Group back towards the northeast. The Liberandos are instructed to attack "targets of opportunity."

9. Around 1155hrs, the trailing groups led by Kane's 98th Group reach IP1 at Piteşti. The 389th Group splits off from the other two groups to conduct its separate mission against Target Red at Câmpina, north of Ploesti.

10. Around noon, Col Jack Wood, commanding the 389th Group, makes the same mistaken turn at IP2 at Târgovişte. He is quickly corrected by other pilots and navigators. He makes an abrupt turn northward, to strike at Target Red at Câmpina. The elaborate three-pronged approach to the target area is abandoned.

11. Shortly before noon, Baker's 93rd Bomb Group attacks the refineries on the southwest corner of Ploesti, and makes an abrupt 108-degree turn to exit the area.

12. Kane's 98th Group and Johnson's 44th Group arrive at IP3 over Floreşti and make a 90-degree turn to the southeast along the railway tracks to start their bomb run.

13. Confused by Compton's approach to Bucharest with the 376th Group, Pitcairn dispatches his reserve force of Bf 110 night fighters to patrol the area northwest of the capital.

14. Maj Norman Appold spots the Concordia Vega refinery at the northwest corner of Ploesti and leads a flight of five B-24 bombers from the 376th Group to attack this target, the only Liberando bombers to actually attack a refinery that day.

15. With the 98th Group on the left (east) and 44th Group on the right (west), the two groups bomb their targets.

16. A portion of the 44th Group led by Lt Col Jim Posey attacks Target Blue, the Creditul Minier refinery near Brazi around 1215hrs.

17. The 389th Group makes its pass down the Prahova valley, striking Target Red on the east side of Câmpina starting at 1213hrs.

Tidal Wave Strikes Ploesti
August 1, 1943

17

3

3

12

7

1

15

14

11

16

2

2

KEY

✈ Airfield

◎ Location of radar station

USAAF Units ●
1. 389th Group
2. 93rd Group
3. 376th Group
4. 98th Group
5. 44th Group

Axis Units ●
1. Esc. 45 Vt (IAR 80)
2. Grupul 6 (IAR 80)
3. I./JG.4 (Bf 109)
4. Bf 110 reserve force

A dramatic view of three B-24D bombers passing over the outskirts of Ploesti. The identity of these aircraft is not recorded, but they may have been the Flying Circus as they passed by the city.

By the time of Appold's attack, most of the rest of the Liberandos had left the immediate Ploesti area and passed south of Câmpina before turning to head home. In the process, they flew under the 98th and 44th Group during the start of their bomb run into Ploesti. Aside from "Brewery Wagon" on its lonesome and heroic mission, no Liberando bombers were lost over Ploesti.

The Liberandos' target, the Română Americana refinery, was not damaged at all during the attack. In fact, its production increased in August 1943 to 109,000 metric tons from 60,000 metric tons in July 1943 to make up for the losses at other Ploesti refineries. It was an embarrassing performance by the *Tidal Wave*'s lead group.

The Flying Circus against Target White III

Col Addison Baker in "Hell's Wench" led the 93rd Group. The group followed behind Compton's lead formation when it made its mistaken turn towards Bucharest. As soon as the turn was made, navigators aboard several aircraft broke radio silence and pointed out the error. With the turn already under way, Baker felt obliged to maintain the course behind Compton in spite of growing doubts. After six minutes and 20 miles, Ploesti was visible to the left of the group. Baker decided to correct the wrong course, and began making a turn towards the target area. It took several minutes for the 37 bombers to execute this maneuver. Aside from the unexpected course change, the new heading meant that the group would have little chance to hit their intended targets, the Concordia Vega, Standard Petrol, and Unirea Sperantza refineries (Targets White II and White III). Instead, they aimed at the most obvious targets, the refineries on the southwest corner of Ploesti.

"Hell's Wench" was in the lead of the formation and flew towards the nearest refinery, Colombia Aquila. This was one of the first *Tidal Wave* aircraft to face the Flak belt around Ploesti, and it took a horrible pounding on the approach. A Flak hit in the nose injured the bombardier and navigator and started a fire. Another Flak hit to the right wing ruptured a fuel cell and set the inboard engine ablaze. The fuel ignited, and soon the outboard engine was also on fire. Baker salvoed the bombs early in the hopes of leading his group over the refinery. The crippled aircraft lurched upward, perhaps to gain altitude to help the crew escape. At least one crewman leaped from the forward nosewheel doors but the fire-damaged wing buckled. Engulfed in flames, "Hell's Wench" nearly collided with another B-24D whose crew recalled that "flames hid everything in the cockpit. Baker went down after he flew his ship to pieces to get us over the target." The aircraft crashed into the Uzina de Creuzot plant nearby with no survivors. Both Baker and co-pilot Maj John Jerstad were awarded the Medal of Honor posthumously for their determined leadership on this mission.

The aircraft to the left of Baker's, "Euroclydon," piloted by Lt Enoch Porter Jr, took a direct Flak hit in the bomb-bay, igniting the fuel tank there. The aircraft's fuselage broke in half aft the wing due to fire damage, crashing near the village of Plopu to the northeast of Ploesti.

The aircraft following Baker attacked targets on the southwestern side of Ploesti. Lt Nicolas Stampolis, piloting "Jose Carioca," was also hit in the bomb-bay while approaching the Colombia Aquila refinery, with a Romanian IAR 80 striking it repeatedly during a firing pass underneath it. After releasing the bombs, the blazing aircraft became uncontrollable and crashed into a women's prison in the city, killing 61 and wounding another 60 on the ground, the highest civilian casualties of the day. The IAR 80 that shot down "Jose Carioca" may have been piloted by Lt Carol Anastasescu of Esc. 62.

Anastasescu later recalled his actions that day:

A few minutes after noon, we took off on patrol, and we received orders to attack the intruders. We were instructed to descend to 200 meters (650ft). I think we ended up around 500 meters (1,650ft). The ground controller asked us if we saw any "trucks" or "motorcyclists," the code names for bombers and escort fighters. We did not spot anything at first. Finally, we spotted the four-engine bombers. I gave the order to attack in a dive and in a line formation. We strafed a bomber, targeting his engines. We made our return pass under the B-24 even though it was very close to the ground. When we lined up again, it seemed unscathed. We had to make three or four passes before smoke appeared. As I attacked a second bomber I saw from the corner of the eye that the first had smashed into the ground. I hit my second target but everything went so fast that I could not see the impact of my firing. After the firing pass, I felt a serious pain in my left foot and heard a noise from the engine. My aircraft was hit and my leather pants were on fire. With an instinctive gesture, I tried to extinguish the flames but burned my hands. It was a really unbearable pain and I opened the canopy to jump. But I was way too low. I tried to regain altitude but the plane could explode at any second. I was on fire and a stream of gas was blinding me and stinging my eyes. I then saw a bomber somewhat separated from his formation. An idea then crossed my mind. I could very quickly end this unbearable pain. I then turned left and aimed at the bomber. I saw a strong light, I felt a terrible heat and that was all.

The second bomber attacked by Anastasescu's formation was probably Lt William Meehan's "The Lady Jane." This aircraft had already been damaged after hitting a balloon cable prior to reaching Astra Română. Machine gunners on the bomber hit the Romanian fighter, setting it on fire. Observers on the ground saw Anastasescu's IAR 80 fighter, No. 222, crash into

Romanian interceptors over the refineries

Lt Carol Anastasescu of Esc. 62 flew IAR 80-B No. 222 on August 1, 1943, serving with the Esc. 62 Vt. of the 6 Grupul based at Pipera. This particular fighter was from a batch that was intended to be built in the IAR 81 dive bomber configuration, but instead was finished as fighters with a pair of 13.2mm heavy machine guns in addition to the usual four 7.92mm machine guns. The two Pipera squadrons had been patrolling to the southwest of Ploesti since late morning when Tigrul air control ordered them to descend through the overcast to find the low-flying bombers. Anastasescu claimed a B-24D during the early fighting, probably "Jose Carioca" from the 93rd Group. On attacking a second B-24D, probably "The Lady Jane," his fighter was hit by machine-gun fire which started a fuel fire that burst into the cockpit. In desperation, Anastasescu decided to ram the bomber rather than burn alive. He struck the B-24D in the cockpit area, and miraculously survived the collision after being thrown from the aircraft into soft silage in a farm field about 150 feet below.

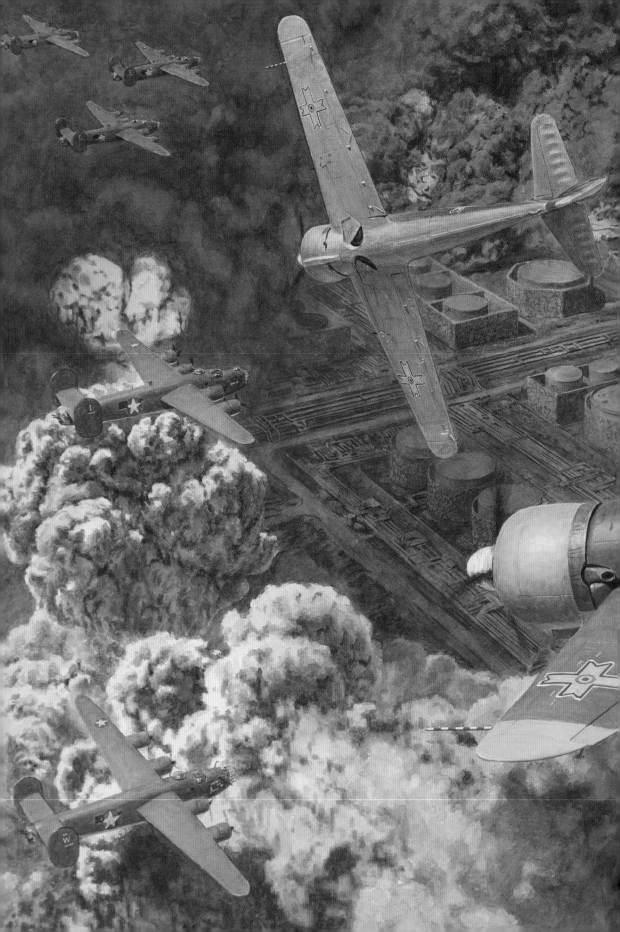

A rare image from film camera footage taken from the cockpit of one of the *Tidal Wave* B-24D bombers moments after a Bf 109G-2 has passed overhead, with the fighter evident in the upper center of the image.

the cockpit area of the B-24. With his canopy open, Anastasescu was thrown clear of his aircraft, falling about 150–200 feet, and landing on a soft pile of silage on the field below. He was found unconscious by Romanian Gendarmes in a sheep meadow near the Concordia Vega refinery and brought to a Ploesti hospital. He remained unconscious for several days before emerging from a coma, still suffering from serious burns.

Lt Hubert Womble's "Honkey Tonk Gal" bombed Colombia Aquila but in the process lost three of its engines to Flak and fire damage. Womble managed to land the aircraft relatively intact near the Ploesti-Târgoviște railway line. Lt Milton Teltser's "Pudgy" lost an engine while attempting to bomb the Astra Română plant. After reaching the eastern side of Ploesti, he turned the aircraft around in the hopes of reaching neutral Turkey. However, "Pudgy" was intercepted by Bf 109 fighters and crash-landed near Ogrezeni, east of Bucharest. Lt Worthy Long aimed his aircraft, "Jersey Bounce 2nd," towards Astra Română. The bomber had already been damaged in a previous fighter attack, and suffered extensive damage by fighters during the bomb run. Further hits from Flak forced Long to crash-land the aircraft near the Vega refinery in Ploieștiori.

Lt Roy Harms' "Hell's Angels" also attacked Astra Română, but was hit by Flak during the approach, losing the left fin and rudder and starting a fuel fire in the bomb-bay. Out of control, the aircraft went into a stall and crashed near Chițorani with only one crewman escaping.

In total, seven of the original 37 aircraft of the 93rd Bomb Group were lost over the immediate target area. The toll would grow larger during the flight back home due to extensive flak damage suffered by the remaining aircraft. Although the group did not hit its intended targets, the bombers did cause damage to various refineries on the southern side of Ploesti.

The attacks on the 93rd Group's intended Target White III were not effective. Only three bombs hit the Standard Petrol Block refinery, and there was no significant damage to

This well known photo of the 344th Squadron, 98th Bomb Group was taken from the waist position of Lt Merrick's "Li'l De-Icer," with Lt Nicholson's "Li'l Jughead" in the foreground to the right and Lt Lewis Ellis' "Daisy Mae" and Lt Dwight Patch's "Black Magic" behind and to the left. The large fireball in the background is believed to be the impact of Lt Ralph Hinch's "Tagalong," which crashed and disintegrated during the attack on Target White IV after being hit by Flak.

the facility. The Unirea Sperantza refinery was not hit, and Concordia Vega was struck by Appold's impromptu raid. The 93rd Group contributed to the damage at Astra Română, but it is impossible to disaggregate their results from those of the subsequent attack by Kane's 98th Group. There was a significant amount of collateral damage to plants in the vicinity of the 93rd Group's attacks including the Concordia Metalurgica plant, Creuzot plant, and a local locomotive depot.

The Pyramidiers at Target White IV

Kane's 98th Group, the Pyramidiers, reached the Danube around 1110hrs and the first IP at Pitești at 1155. By the time that they approached Ploesti, the city was already engulfed in black clouds from initial attacks by Baker's 93rd Group. Instead of attacking an unobscured target, the Pyramidiers would now have to locate and attack their targets through the smoke and flames engulfing the Astra Română refinery. To make matters worse, some of the trailing aircraft from the 93rd Group were still transiting across the intended flight path of the Pyramidiers, threatening inadvertent collisions. The Romanian and German Flak batteries in this sector were on full alert and were ready when Kane's group approached.

At this stage, the 98th Group was down to 40 aircraft due to aborts by six aircraft earlier in the mission. The final approach from the IP at Florești to the target at Ploesti was 13 miles (20km), taking about three minutes. Target White IV, the Astra Română and Unirea Orion refineries, was on the southern side of Ploesti. Kane's Group flew down along one of the main railway lines on the western side of Ploesti. Moving along the rail-line was "Die Raupe," the "Caterpillar" Flak train. Kane's group was engaged by German 20mm cannon on the train as well as Romanian 20mm batteries located on the west side of Ploesti. The gun turrets on the B-24D bombers began engaging the train and any Flak batteries they spotted. Kane later guessed that seven of his bombers were seriously damaged in the brief but furious engagement with the Flak train. Only a few of the aircraft crashed before reaching the target, but several sustained enough damage that they crashed within the refinery or shortly after.

Kane's Eagle Flight arrived in Romania with six of its original ten aircraft; the other four had aborted due to mechanical issues. Kane's lead aircraft, "Hail Columbia," dropped its bombs over White IV at 1213hrs. To Kane's left, Lt Samuel Neeley's "Raunchy" was hit by Flak and struck a balloon cable near the wing-root, ripping off the wing; two crewmen survived the crash. Lt Ralph Hinch's "Tagalong" lost two engines to Flak and ended up crashing in a cornfield south of the refineries; five crewmen survived.

By the time that Maj Herbert Shinger's Fox Flight reached the target, the flames from the burning refineries erupted to heights greater than the 240ft altitude flown by the aircraft. The prop wash from other aircraft and the swirling clouds of smoke and flame made it difficult for the pilots and co-pilots to keep control of the unwieldy bombers. Dodging

One of the most famous images from *Tidal Wave* was taken from the rear camera on "Chug-a-Lug" looking back as B-24D "The Sandman" (42-40402), piloted by Lt Robert Sternfels of the 345th Squadron, 98th Group, passed through a huge plume of black smoke, missing the stacks near the McKee distillation plant at Target White IV, the Astra Română refinery.

Another view of Sternfels' B-24D "The Sandman" as it makes its pass over the Astra Română refinery around 1212hrs at a height of 280 feet.

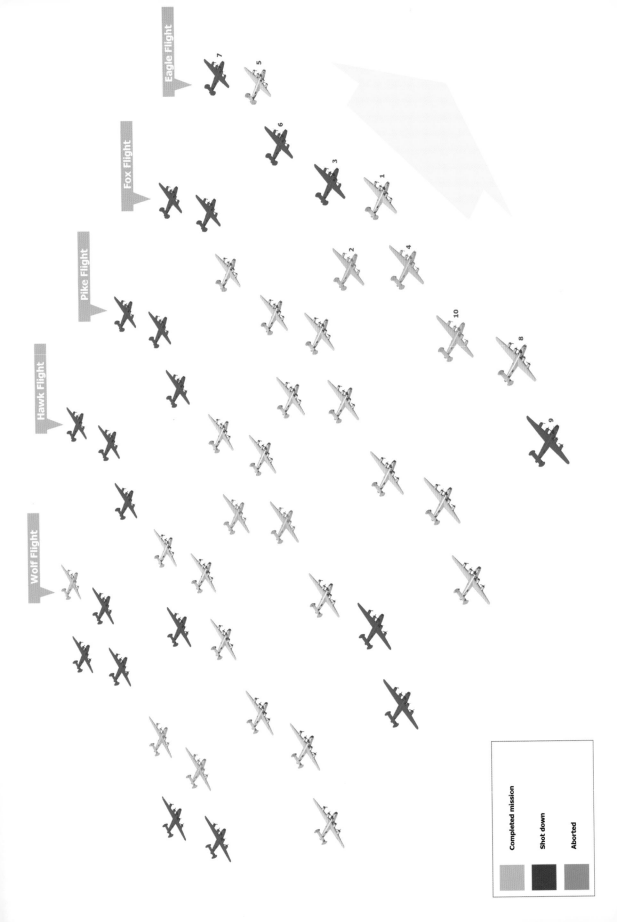

Eagle Flight

Fox Flight

Pike Flight

Hawk Flight

Wolf Flight

Completed mission

Shot down

Aborted

OPPOSITE 98TH BOMB GROUP "THE PYRAMIDIERS" ATTACK FORMATION

Flight	#	Pilot	Name	Fate
Eagle	1	Col John Kane	Hail Columbia	Returned Cyprus
	2	Lt Herbert Arens	Rosie Wrecked 'Em	Aborted
	3	Lt Gilbert Hadley	Hadley's Harem	Crashed off Turkish coast
	4	Lt Allen Gaston	Rowdy II	Aborted
	5	Lt William Banks	Sad Sack	Returned Cyprus
	6	Lt Samuel Neeley	Raunchy	Shot down
	7	Lt Ralph Hinch	Tagalong	Shot down
	8	Lt Royden Lebrecht	The Squaw	Returned Libya
	9	Lt Robert Nespor	Kickapoo	Crashed
	10	Lt Hoover Edwards	Big Operator	Aborted
Fox	1	Maj Herbert Shingler	Fertile Myrtle	Returned Benghazi
	2	Lt James Merrick	Lil' De-Icer	Returned Benghazi
	3	Lt Robert Nicholson	Lil' Jughead	Returned Benghazi
	4	Lt Lewis Ellis	Daisy Mae	Returned Benghazi
	5	Lt Ned McCarty	Cornhusker	Shot down, Ionian Sea
	6	Lt Dwight Patch	Black Magic	Returned Benghazi
	7	Lt Theodore Helin	Boiler Maker II	Shot down
	8	Lt Wesley Pettigrew	Lil' Joe	Returned Benghazi
	9	Lt Andrew Opsata	Stinger	Returned Benghazi
	10	Lt Martin Speiser	Penelope	Returned Benghazi
Pike	1	Lt Col Julian Bleyer	Nightmare	Returned Benghazi
	2	Capt Thomas Bennett	Prince Charming	Aborted
	3	Lt Glen Underwood	Northern Star	Returned Benghazi
	4	Lt Carl Looker	Shanghai Lil	Aborted
	5	Lt Clarence Gooden	Unnamed	Shot down
	6	Lt Lawrence Murphy	Boots	Shot down
	7	Lt Lawrence Hadcock	Four Eyes	Shot down
	8	Capt James Gunn	Snow White and the Seven Dwarves	Shot down, Bulgaria
	9	Lt Julian Darlington	The Witch	Shot down, Bulgaria
	10	Lt Donald Johnson	Sneezy	Returned Benghazi
Hawk	1	Maj Delbert Hahn	Black Jack	Returned Libya
	2	Lt Thomas Fravega	Chief	Returned Sicily
	3	Lt John Ward	Maternity Ward	Shot down, Ionian Sea
	4	Lt Lindley Hussey	Lil' Joe	Shot down
	5	Lt John Dore	Old Baldy	Shot down
	6	Lt John Thomas	Aire Lobo	Shot down
	7	Lt Hilary Blevins	Snake Eyes	Landed Sicily
	8	Lt Leroy Morgan	Chug-a-Lug	Returned Benghazi
	9	FO Charles Salyer	Battle Axe	Returned Benghazi
	10	Lt Robert Sternfels	The Sandman	Returned Libya
Wolf	1	Capt Wallace Taylor	Vulgar Virgin	Shot down
	2	Lt James Deeds	-	Shot down
	3	Lt Francis Weisler	Baby	Aborted
	4	Lt Edward McGuire	Yen Tu	Shot down
	5	Capt George Colchagoff	Skipper	Aborted
	6	Lt James Haverty	Edna Elizabeth	Aborted
	7	Lt John McGraw	Jersey Jackass	Shot down
	8	Lt August Sulflow	Semper Felix	Shot down

A view from "Chug-a-Lug" of the 98th Group passing over the burning boiler house and distillation plant of the Astra Română refinery after it had been set alight by the 93rd Group.

the various stacks and towers of the refineries forced the pilots to make violent maneuvers. "Boiler Maker II" flown by Lt Ted Helin lost two engines to Flak, but made it about six miles beyond the refinery before crash landing. Nine of the ten bombers of this formation survived the bomb run.

The third wave, Lt Col Julian Bleyer's Pike Wing, was hit hard. Bleyer's bomber "Nightmare" was near the center of the eight-plane formation; all three aircraft to his right were lost to Flak. "Four Eyes," flown by Lt Lawrence Hadcock, had been hit during the approach to target and crashed before reaching the Unirea Orion refinery with all its crew killed. "Boots," flown by Lt Lawrence Murphy, took a Flak hit in the bomb-bay and crashed into the cracking plant; the two waist gunners survived. "Margie" flown by Lt Clarence Gooden was hit by Flak and crashed in the refinery with two crewmen surviving.

Maj Delbert Hahn's Hawk Flight was the fourth wave with ten bombers. Of these, "Lil Joe," piloted by Lt Lindsey Hussey, was leaking fuel in the bomb-bay on the approach, and a Flak hit started a conflagration in the bomb-bay. Hussey tried to pull up beyond the refinery to permit the crew to parachute, with six jumping and three surviving. The plane exploded and crashed. "Old Baldy" flown by Lt John Dore Jr was hit by Flak and crashed into the Romanian 88mm gun Bateria Nr. 86, killing the entire aircraft crew as well as six of the gun crew. "Aire Lobo" flown by Lt John Thomas had been hit by Flak on the approach and then suffered another Flak hit in the cockpit over the target. The aircraft impacted on its left wing and disintegrated; the navigator was thrown clear of the wreck and was the only survivor from the crew. During the bomb run, at least two Romanian IAR 80 piloted by av. Criste Cristu and av. Bosinceanu attacked the formation, striking the top turret of "Chug-a-Lug" piloted by Lt Leroy Morgan and killing the gunner.

The fifth and final wave of the 98th Group, Capt Wallace Taylor's Wolf Flight, entered the refinery area with only six aircraft. This formation was wiped out but for one aircraft; Taylor's "Vulgar Virgin" was hit in the nose by Flak on the approach. He attempted to gain altitude and ordered the crew to bail out. Four managed to get out of the bomber before

B-24D (41-11766) "Chug-a-Lug" from the 345th Squadron, 98th Group was piloted by Lt Leroy Morgan over Ploesti, and was heavily damaged with one crewman killed and two others wounded. Many of the iconic photos of the raid were photographed from this aircraft, including the photos of "The Sandman" emerging from the smoke over Target White IV. This aircraft survived 105 missions and was sent back to the United States for a war bonds drive in July 1944.

the crash, but only Taylor survived. The unnamed B-24D flown by Lt James Deeds took a Flak hit in the cockpit area over the target, starting a fire in the bomb-bay which led to the disintegration of the aircraft; the co-pilot was blown out of the wreckage and miraculously survived. "Yen Tu" flown by Lt Edward McGuire had already been hit by Flak during the approach and was on fire from the bomb-bay area when entering the target zone. McGuire tried to gain altitude after the bomb run to permit the crew to parachute but only three escaped before the aircraft crashed near Bărcănești. "Semper Felix" flown by Lt August Sulflow had been hit by Flak on the bomb run and crashed shortly beyond the refinery with only one survivor. "Jersey Jackass" flown by Lt John McGraw was hit by Flak that ignited the bomb-bay area. The aircraft reached as far as the Berceni area before crashing with four escaping the wreck; McGraw died later from his burns. "Baby" flown by Lt Francis Weisler was trailing the rest of the flight after losing an engine to Flak on the approach. It was the last aircraft of the Pyramidiers over the refinery, and the sole survivor of the six-ship flight.

B-24D (41-11819) "Raunchy" from the 344th Squadron, 98th Group was piloted by Lt Samuel Neeley. This aircraft was immediately left of Kane's "Hail Columbia" over the refinery when it struck a balloon cable and lost its wing, with only two crewmen escaping.

In total, 14 bombers of the original 40 B-24D bombers of the 98th Group that had reached the target area were shot down in the immediate vicinity of Ploesti, the heaviest losses suffered by any group during the *Tidal Wave* attacks.

Later US assessments estimated that the attacks on Target White IV by Baker's 93rd and Kane's 98th Groups placed 50 bombs on the Astra Română refinery. At Astra Română, the furnaces of the McKee plant were badly damaged. The pump house at the Shell stills and Dubbs cracking plant were both hit. The cracked-gasoline stabilizer building, the doctor plant, and the agitator building were damaged. Battery 1 was repaired in 12 days, and the McKee unit resumed operations a month later on September 1. The cracking coils were back on line by September 8. An initial Romanian report indicated that the attack cut production in half. Overall, the raid caused the loss of 68,000 metric tons of fuel production in August. However, September output exceeded July output due to excess capacity at the massive refinery.

The bombing of the Orion refinery damaged the Still pipe installation, the power plant, steam plant, the pump house, and three fuel cars. The Romanians reported that it suffered a short-term loss of 70 percent of its capacity.

B-24D (41-11761) "The Squaw" from the 344th Squadron, 98th Group was piloted by Lt Royden Lebrecht. Low on fuel, this bomber followed Kane's "Hail Columbia" to Cyprus. It is seen here for dispatch to the United States for a war-bond drive with its battle-damage identified with prominent patches.

A view looking south over Target White V, the Colombia Aquila refinery identifying (1) the stabilization plant, (2) the distillation plant, (3) the boiler house, and (4) the pumping station. Further south are Targets White III and White IV. This photo was taken during a 1944 attack from an aircraft flying higher than the *Tidal Wave* attackers.

In view of the heavy losses suffered while attacking this refinery, the results were extremely disappointing. The poor results were in some measure due to the unexpected attack on the refinery by the 93rd Group which started numerous fires, complicating the target run of the 98th Group.

The Flying 8-Balls at Target White V

The 44th Group was assigned two targets: the Colombia Aquila refinery (Target White V) on the southwest side of Ploesti and the Creditul Minier refinery (Target Blue) in Brazi to the south of Ploesti. Col Leon Johnson in "Suzy Q" led a detachment of 16 bombers against White V while Lt Col Jim Posey led the other waves of the 44th Group against Target Blue.

Johnson's detachment from the 66th Bomb Squadron, 44th Group headed for White V to the right side of Kane's 98th Group. This formation endured far fewer Flak hits than Kane's. Nevertheless, several bombers were damaged during the approach. Johnson's detachment was over the Colombia Aquila refinery at 1213hrs. On the way out of the target, the lead wave was attacked by fighters, including at least one Bf 110 night fighter. The second wave was also hit by an attack by between five and seven Bf 109 fighters, probably from JG.4. The machine gunners on the bombers claimed to have shot down one Bf 109 and three Ju 88 (Bf 110 night fighters) in this engagement. The B-24D piloted by Worden Weaver left the target area with one inoperative engine and two more on fire due to Flak. The Bf 109s pounced on this straggler and it crash-landed in a cornfield about 30 miles south of Ploesti. The third wave of bombers in this detachment took particularly heavy losses to Flak and fighters during the approach and the bomb run over White V.

One of the last planes over the target, "Wing Dinger," piloted by Lt George Winger, was hit by Flak

An image taken from a rear-mounted camera on B-24D "Suzy Q" of the 67th Squadron, 44th Group passing over the Colombia Aquila refinery with more than a dozen Liberators approaching on the horizon. The fires evident here were caused by the earlier bombing of the refinery by the 93rd Group. "Suzy Q" was the command ship of Col Leon Johnson on this mission.

that set fire to the nose compartment. Shouting back to the crew to get out, Winger and co-pilot Edward Barnett attempted to gain altitude after exiting the target to give the crew enough height to parachute. The plane went into a hammerhead stall and crashed. Three crewmen exited the aircraft before it crashed, but only two survived. Romanian accounts suggest that this aircraft was also hit by the IAR 80 of Esc. 45 Vt. piloted by Ioan Barladeanu.

Barladeanu was one of two IAR 80 pilots credited with downing two bombers that day. After having hit "Wing Dinger," Barladeanu apparently attacked the B-24D piloted by Lt Henry Lasco that had already taken a Flak hit in the radio compartment. Barladeanu later recalled the day's fighting:

Another image from Suzy Q's rear-mounted camera during the attack on the Colombia Aquila refinery by the 44th Group. This provides a good view of the way in which the German engineers fortified the refinery with blast walls around many critical components to reduce bomb and fire damage.

Suddenly, ahead of us but much lower, I saw a huge number of enemy four-motor bombers with the sun glistening off their wings. I held back a cry of surprise. I radioed my wingman (Diditza) if he saw the same thing. Affirmative, he replied and he asked me what he should do. I ordered him to wait a moment to prepare the attack. We had the sun in the back and had a much higher altitude. I carefully studied the formations and it seemed that I had hundreds of machines in front of me with their bellies full of bombs. I had never seen such an imposing formation; it seemed to me to extend for tens of kilometers ... In front of the enemy bombers, there was a dense wall of smoke and explosions. Our antiaircraft artillery was firing at them. I announced the attack to Diditza and then threw my fighter into a dive, quickly increasing the speed of my IAR. I stormed into the first wave of bombers. I fired my guns, crunching my head down, relying on the armor of my seat to shield me. Tracers were flying everywhere. I did not care about choosing a specific target and shot at everything that appeared. I then got a single bomber into my viewfinder and fired a burst when I was 400 meters away. The aim point of my sight was to the inside left of an engine. I pressed the firing button until my hand hurt. A long and continuous burst. I saw the explosion of my tracers on the engine, and it began to spit out fire and smoke. The four-engine flew a few more seconds and then stalled before crashing. I could not believe he had crashed. My God! I was overwhelmed by emotion. I felt a nervous tremor throughout my body and my teeth chattered uncontrollably. My wingman was zig-zagging between streams of projectiles spewed by the enemy machine guns. His IAR 80 finally appeared on my right, like a pair of crazy birds in a storm. The sky was streaked with lines of tracers and studded with black, white, and brown Flak bursts. On the ground below, detonations, flames, and debris on fire. The bombs exploded continuously creating enormous eruptions of flames, and columns of smoke rising higher and higher. A B-24 vanished under the fire of a neighboring IAR 80, falling from the formation like a disoriented swallow. My wingman and I climbed higher in wide spirals to restart the attack. This time I did not feel the fear anymore. Maybe I was going to have a second chance? A projectile ricocheted off my fuselage, and then I saw a four-engine aircraft in front of me, barely 200 meters away. Its engines were approaching very fast in my viewfinder, and the propellers seemed to be spinning very, very slowly. Calmly, I pulled the control stick and dodged it. The sky was filled with planes. I began to pursue a bomber flying in the same direction as me and opened fire. Two bursts were enough. The fire struck his wing and reached one of his gas tanks. In a few seconds, the four-engine was completely engulfed in flames. I was speechless. It took me only a few seconds to win this second victory.

B-24D (41-24226) served at Ploesti with the name "Utah Man," piloted by Lt Walter Stewart of the 330th Squadron, 93rd Bomb Group. This aircraft had 376 holes after Tidal Wave, was repaired and renamed as "Joisey Bounce" as seen here. It was lost on November 13, 1943 on a mission to Bremen, Germany when it collided with another aircraft.

Barladeanu's firing pass killed the engineer and tail gunner as well as knocking out one engine. Lasco managed to crash-land the bomber in a corn field near Butimanu and four of the crew including Lasco survived. Of the 16 planes from Johnson's detachment of the 44th Group attacking White V, five were shot down in the immediate area of Ploesti.

The attacks caused severe damage to the refinery. A bomb hit the pump house of the distillation unit causing extensive damage. Another direct hit severed the Lachman Tresting tower from the cracking unit. The bubble tower and gas-oil accumulator were knocked off their foundations. The absorber column of the stabilization plant was severed at three places by bomb hits. In 1943 the Colombia Aquila refinery had processed 34,000 metric tons of fuel prior to *Tidal Wave*, but the damage was so extensive that the plant was shut down for a year, not returning to service until August 1944.

The Flying 8-Balls at Target Blue

The second detachment of 20 B-24D bombers from the 68th Bomb Squadron, 44th Group was led by Lt Col James Posey, flying "Victory Ship." Their objective was Target Blue, the Creditul Minier refinery to the south of Ploesti near Brazi. Their target was the southernmost of the *Tidal Wave* attacks and it took about five minutes to fly from the final

B-24D "Jerk's Natural" of the 409th Squadron, 93rd Group piloted by Lt Harold Kendall at Ploesti. Although assigned to Target White III, this aircraft bombed Target White V. The crew claimed to have shot down one IAR 80 during the mission. The national insignia on the fuselage side has had the white star subdued with a wash of gray paint and the yellow around the roundel overpainted.

The 44th Group exits Target Blue at Brazi with the sky obscured by sooty black clouds from the burning refinery and white chemical smoke near the ground from the German smoke generators.

IP at Floreşti to the target, most of the time within range of the Romanian and German Flak batteries. The lead wave of the formation reached Target Blue with modest damage, and the bombers used the approach flight to machine-gun enemy Flak positions. On leaving the target, Capt Rowland Houston's "Satan's Hell Cats" was streaming smoke from one of its engines, and then attacked by a Bf 109G-2 piloted by Hauptmann Wilhelm Steinmann of 1./JG 4. Gunners on the bomber managed to hit the German fighter, and both aircraft crashed near Brazi. This was the second B-24D shot down that day by Steinmann.

The second wave led by Capt Reginald Philips in "Lemon Drop" was also hit by fighters on the way out of the target, with "Avenger" claiming to have downed two Bf 109s and a Bf 110. This wave escaped with several damaged aircraft but no losses in the immediate Ploesti area.

Escadrila 53 Vt., the Romanian Bf 109G-2 squadron based at Mizil, had been sent on a wild goose chase on its first mission, but returned to base for refueling. On its second mission, it caught some of the last B-24D bombers departing from the area south of Ploesti, probably from the 44th Group. Two of the fighters were hit by machine gun fire from the bombers, but two of the fighters, piloted by Lt. Ion Maga and av. Dumitru Encioiu were credited with one bomber each.

The center aircraft in the fourth and final wave, "GI Gal," piloted by Lt Elmer Reinhart, took several Flak hits, knocking out one engine and setting a wing fuel cell ablaze. The bomber endured fighter attacks, and came near to crashing while exiting the target area.

Deadly duel over Brazi

Hauptmann Wilhelm Steinmann from the Stab (headquarters flight) of JG.4 was nicknamed "Onkel Willi" (Uncle Willi) in his unit because he was 30 years old, so much older than most of the other pilots. He was originally a bomber pilot and converted to fighters in 1942. He was serving with 3./JG 27 on the English Channel when, on June 1, 1943, he mistakenly shot down a Bf 109G-6 flown by the Gruppenkommandeur of I./JG 27, Hauptmann Erich Hohagen, an ace with 56 victories. Steinmann was exiled to Romania as punishment. On August 1, he claimed a B-24D south of Ploesti in fighter grid SN1 around 1204hrs. As depicted here, he subsequently attacked "Satan's Hell Cats," piloted by Capt Rowland Houston. Steinmann managed to shoot down the bomber, but in the process his fighter was hit by machine-gun fire from the top and rear turrets and he crashed near Brazi around 1230hrs, not far from the wreck of "Satan's Hell Cats."

B-24D "Lemon Drop" (41-23699) of the 68th Squadron, 44th Group piloted by Capt Reginald Philips was the lead ship of the second wave attacking Target Blue and survived the *Tidal Wave* mission.

Reinhardt managed to keep the aircraft flying for a further 95 miles, but the damage was too severe. The crew bailed out near Piatra, with all but one crewman surviving.

Of the 20 bombers attacking Target Blue, only one was lost in the immediate target area, and a second less than a half-hour afterwards due to damage incurred during the attack. This attack proved to be one of the best executed of the day. The damage to the Creditul Minier refinery was extensive and this refinery was shut down and never resumed production during the war. A total of 59 high-explosive bombs and about 90 incendiaries impacted this refinery. One strike near the primary distillation tower started a large fire that buckled the distillation column and rendered it unrepairable. A direct hit and a near miss demolished the pipe-still furnace. The cracking plant received extensive but repairable damage and could have been

B-24D (42-40619) of the 566th Squadron, 389th Group was piloted by Capt Emery Ward and carried section commander Maj John Brooks during the *Tidal Wave* mission. It survived the Ploesti mission but was lost on a mission over Gotha, Germany on February 24, 1944.

returned to work in two months. However, the damage to the pipe-still rendered this effort unproductive. The pump house of the casing-head stabilizing plant suffered a direct hit, and the subsequent fire destroyed much of the facility. The refinery's electrical generators were put out of action by hits on the power plant and the boiler house. The loss of this refinery trimmed about 45,000 metric tons of monthly capacity from the Ploesti output.

Scorpions at Target Red

The 389th Group was assigned Target Red, the Steaua Română refinery at Câmpina, north of Ploesti. The formation commander, Col Jack Wood, flew onboard "The Scorpion" piloted by Capt Kenneth Caldwell. The 29 bombers of the 389th separated from the 44th and 98th Groups at Pitești, with about 42 miles to the target area. The Sky Scorpions ran into navigation problems due to low clouds and haze. An important landmark was the Monastera Dealului, but it could not be seen. Col Wood attempted to estimate the turn based on elapsed time and instructed Caldwell to turn up a valley that appeared to be running in the proper direction. The navigator complained that the turn was wrong, and "The Scorpion" led the Group on a confusing 180 degree turn after realizing their mistake.

The attack plan for Target Red was more complicated than most of the other targets, with the Group expected to break up into three detachments, each made of up of two to five elements of three aircraft each. The intention was to attack the four main objectives in the refinery, the two distilling plants, boiler house and cracking plant, from three directions by multiple aircraft in separate passes. The Câmpina area was not as heavily defended as Ploesti and casualties to Flak were markedly lower. Lt Robert O'Reilly's "Chattanooga Choo-Choo" was hit by Flak. Before he could ditch the aircraft, the crew warned O'Reilly that a remaining bomb had remained lodged in the slings in the bomb-bay. The crew managed to jettison the bomb, and O'Reilly landed the crippled aircraft in a river bed.

As the subsequent waves of aircraft passed over the target, the Romanian and German flak fire increased in intensity. Lt Lloyd "Pete" Hughes' "Ole Kickapoo" was hit by Flak on the

B-24D (42-40743) piloted by Lt Dale Sisson of the 567th Squadron, 389th Group was one of the survivors of the Ploesti mission and is seen here in Britain after returning to the Eighth Air Force.

A departing view of the Target Red, the Steaua Roman refinery at Câmpina, as the 389th Group exits the area. The smoke is rising from the damaged boiler house and power station in the refinery.

approach with a stream of gas coming from gaps in the left wing fuel cells. Neighboring pilots warned him about the encroaching fire. Hughes acknowledged over the radio by insisted that "I gotta get the bombs on target." After successfully dropping the bombs, Hughes and his co-pilot attempted to crash-land the burning aircraft on a river bed. The damage was too severe, and the plane cartwheeled when it hit the ground. Four crewmen managed to escape the wreck, but two died of wounds and burns. Hughes was later awarded the Medal of Honor for his valiant effort to keep his plane in formation to complete the mission.

The third aircraft lost during the attack was "Sand-Witch" piloted by Lt Robert Horton. The bomb-bay fuel tank was apparently punctured by Flak and then ignited by flames from the burning refinery when the aircraft passed over the target. Horton attempted a crash landing in the river bed beyond the target area, but the aircraft disintegrated on landing. Three crewmen escaped the wreckage but two died of their injuries.

Although only three aircraft were lost in the immediate target area, several other bombers had suffered significant damage from the Flak batteries. "Boomerang," piloted by Lt Melvin Neef, lost two engines due to Flak damage. Neef attempted a belly landing at Butoiu about 40 miles from Câmpina. The aircraft was heavily damaged during the landing attempt, but all the crewmen survived.

During the Câmpina attack, the fourth element was attacked by Romanian night fighters. B-24D "Todelao" piloted by Lt Cecil Whitener fought back and the top turret gunner, SSgt Lawson, is believed to have hit the Bf 110C piloted by Cpt. av. Marin Chica that subsequently crashed near Roşiorii de Vede.

The Câmpina strike was the most accurate and successful attack of the *Tidal Wave* mission, with heavy damage inflicted on the target and relatively modest losses suffered by the attack force. A total of 74 bombs hit the refinery according to US assessments. Romanian reports indicate that this was an underestimate and that in fact 131 high explosive bombs had hit the refinery of which 11 were duds. Roughly 2,000 incendiaries were dropped of which 500 failed to ignite. Both Stratford distillation units were severely damaged. The main column of the McKee unit was cut in half by a direct hit, and the control house was badly damaged by the subsequent fires. The older Shell still battery suffered damage, while the oil treating plant including the paraffin plant were destroyed by fire. The boiler house and electrical generator were hit and damaged. The refinery had processed 44,000 metric tons of fuel in July 1943 but was put out of operation until January 1944. It never completely recovered from the attack, and was subsequently shut down by USAAF bombing in May 1944.

The return trip

The *Tidal Wave* plan included an elaborate scheme for the five groups to rally together after the oil field strike and return to Libya as a coherent force. In view of the casualties and the ragged state of many of the groups, the return trip was chaotic. Some formations did return in relatively good order, but many of the bombers headed away from Ploesti

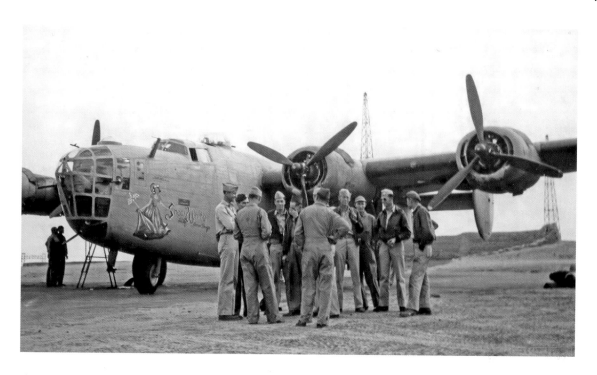

alone or in small groups. Due to damage, some crews feared they could not make it back to Libya and decided instead on alternate landing places, including neutral Turkey. The planned path back to Libya followed much the same course as the inbound flight, briefly skirting through northwest Bulgaria, across Serbia and Albania, and out in the Ionian and Mediterranean Seas.

As mentioned earlier, the Bulgarian air force had scrambled their fighters of the 6th Fighter Regiment during the inbound flight, but had failed to make an intercept. On the return flight, Jäfu Bulgarien had much better information on the timing of the flight, and so was able to put fighter squadrons in the path of the incoming bombers. This time, seven Avia B.534 Dogan biplane fighters from Bozhurishche, four B.534 from Vrazhdebna airbase, and four Bf 109G-2 Strela were sent aloft to intercept the intruders.

"Snow White and the Seven Dwarves" (42-40364) of the 343rd Squadron, 98th Bomb Group, piloted by Capt James Gunn III, survived the Ploesti attack but was shot down by a Bulgarian Bf 109G-2 piloted by Lt Petar Bochev over Skopje, with the loss of the entire crew but one.

"Cornhusker" (42-40322) of the 415th Squadron, 98th Group was piloted by Lt Ned McCarty. It survived the attack on Ploesti only to be shot down during the return flight over the Ionian Sea by the Bf 109G-2 of Oblt Ernst-Georg Altnorthoff from 12./JG.27, with no survivors.

The crew led by pilot Lt Reginald Carpenter flying B-24D (41-24042) "Bewitching Witch" of the 512th Squadron, 44th Group. Although the aircraft survived the Ploesti bomb run, it was shot down by Bf 109G-2 fighters of the 12./JG.27 in the Ionian Sea late in the afternoon while returning to Libya. Carpenter managed to belly-land the aircraft and seven of the nine-man crew survived. Their life raft was spotted by an RAF Wellington on maritime patrol around dawn on August 2, and they were rescued by an RAF launch that evening.

The obsolete B.534 fighters had a difficult task reaching high altitude in time but did manage to conduct a number of firing passes, mainly against bombers of the 98th Group. Their slow speed relative to the bombers meant that most fighters were able to conduct only a single pass before the bombers flew away. Another significant problem was that the light machine gun armament of the B.534 was not adequate to cause fatal damage to the B-24. As a result, no B-24 was lost to the biplane fighters and some of the Bulgarian biplanes were damaged. The four Bf 109G-2 fighters, led by Por. Stoyan Stoyanov, encountered the bombers over Ferdinand and Varshek. During the intercept, Stoyanov claimed two B-24 shot down. Two other pilots, Petr Bonev and Kristo Krystev, claimed one each. Among the casualties to the Bulgarian fighter attack were three B-24 bombers from the 98th Group, "The Witch," "Snow White and the Seven Dwarves," and "Prince Charming." Four crewmen from "The Witch" escaped capture and joined the Yugoslav partisans. Bulgarian antiaircraft batteries claimed three more. In total, the Bulgarian air force launched 35 sorties on August 1 against *Tidal Wave*, 21 with the B.534 Dogan fighters and 14 with the Bf 109G-2.

Hostile fighters were not the only problem. On reaching the mountains, some of the bombers encountered thick cloud cover. Two bombers of the 330th Squadron, 93rd Group, "Exterminator" and "Let 'er Rip," collided over Brod, Serbia with all but three crewmen killed.

Col John "Killer" Kane's command ship, "Hail Columbia," had been badly damaged and Kane led a small contingent of damaged bombers of the 98th Group south across Bulgaria and Turkey to Cyprus.

The bulk of the returning Liberators, flying the planned path through Serbia and Albania, had a final gauntlet to run when they reached the Ionian Sea. Jäfu Balkan in Serbia had monitored the return flight using radars on the mountain tops in the Dinaric Alps. The command center radioed ahead to III./Jagdgeschwader.27, stationed at Kalamaki/Tanagara airbase on the Greek coast. The Bf 109G-2 fighters began to intercept the bombers about 25 miles (40km) west of the island of Kefalonia at an altitude of 3,300 feet (1,000m), starting

B-24D "Hadley's Harem," piloted by Lt Gilbert Hadley from the 344th Squadron, 98th Group, received Flak damage over the refinery, killing the bombardier and damaging one engine. After passing over Turkey, two engines failed and Hadley tried to land in Turkey. However, the aircraft crashed on the Mediterranean coast and seven crewmen survived. Both the pilot and co-pilot were unable to escape the sinking aircraft. A large portion of the aircraft was later recovered and it is currently on display at the Rahmi M. Koç Museum in Istanbul, the sole surviving aircraft of Operation *Tidal Wave*. (Richard Griffith)

around 1530hrs. The first bomber shot down was "Available Jones" of the 67th Squadron, 44th Group piloted by Lt Fred Jones and claimed by Fw Ernst Hackl of 12./JG.27. This was quickly followed by Lt Ned McCarty's "Cornhusker" of the 98th Group, claimed by Oblt Ernst-Georg Altnorthoff, also from 12./JG.27. The third Liberator to fall was Maj Ralph McBride's "Here's To Ya" of the 93rd Group, hit by the Bf 109G-2 of Uffz Rudolf Philipp. By this stage, the fighters were running low on fuel and returned to base. The Bf 109G-2 of Uffz Max Graf from 10./JG.27 was shot down over the Ionian Sea by machine gun fire from the bombers.

A second sortie by 11./JG.27 and the HQ flight encountered the bombers again about 1700hrs. A fourth bomber, Lt Reginald Carpenter's "Bewitching Witch" of the 512th Squadron, 44th Group, lost an engine to the fighters but staggered along some distance before crashing. The final claim was made by Leutnant Hans Flor, who intercepted and shot down a straggler about 125 miles (200km) north of Benghazi around 1713hrs; Graf's aircraft was damaged and crashed on landing in Greece. This was the last loss of a *Tidal Wave* aircraft to enemy fighters.

The first bombers began returning back at Benghazi at 1720hrs. Of the attack force, 89 aircraft completed the 14-hour, 2,400-mile trip back to base in Benghazi, Libya. A total of 54 bombers of the original 178 were lost, of which 41 were credited

Officers and enlisted men of the IX Bomber Command watch as the first B-24D bombers return from *Tidal Wave* in the early evening of August 1, 1943. The women in the photo are from Jack Benny's visiting USO entertainment troupe.

Ninth Air Force commander, Maj Gen Lewis Brereton, on the left, headed out to greet mission commander Brig Gen Uzal Ent after command ship "Teggie Ann" had returned to Benghazi. Ent had sent a misleading message "Mission successful" to Brereton hours earlier. To the right, the dejected look on the face of Col K. K. Compton suggests otherwise.

to enemy action, six to operational causes including collisions and mechanical problems, and seven landed in neutral Turkey where their crews were interned. A total of 13 B-24D had mechanical problems and had aborted the mission earlier in the morning, returning to Benghazi. A further 28 returned to alternate bases in Allied hands, including nine on Sicily, seven on Malta, and 12 on Cyprus. Of the returning aircraft, 55 had suffered significant damage. Of the 1,753 crewmen who embarked on *Tidal Wave*, 516 did not return, including 132 captured in Romania and Bulgaria and 76 interned in Turkey.

An exhausted crew from a B-24 of the 376th Group moves down a chow-line at Benghazi on the evening of August 1, 1943 following the *Tidal Wave* mission.

ANALYSIS

In the immediate aftermath of the *Tidal Wave* raid, both sides felt that they had secured a significant victory. During the return flight back to Benghazi on the afternoon of August 1, 1943, Gen Ent aboard "Teggie Ann" sent a terse radio message back to Brereton in Benghazi "MS," the code for "Mission Successful." His assessment would be debated for many years.

B-24J bombers of the Fifteenth Air Force attack the Concordia Vega refinery during the mission A67 of May 31, 1944. This mission included 53 B-17 and 42 B-24 bombers dropping 1,115.6 tons of bombers. A total of 16 bombers were lost on this mission, with 13 lost to Flak.

IX Bomber Command casualties, August 1, 1943					
	Bombers lost	**Bombers interned**	**KIA/ MIA**	**PoW/ Interned**	**Total casualties**
44th Group	9	2	43	50	93
93rd Group	11	2	90	47	137
98th Group	21	-	144	51	195
376th Group	2	1	12	18	30
389th Group	4	2	19	42	61
Total	47	7	308	208	516

In view of the heavy losses suffered by IX Bomber Command over Ploesti, there was an understandable tendency to laud the heroism of the crews and to extol the accomplishments of the mission. The initial reports to the press suggested that the Ploesti raid had caused severe setbacks to the German war effort.

Internal USAAF assessment made a more critical appraisal of the raid, but it took some time before enough data was collected to reach any firm conclusions. The commander of the Ninth Air Force, Gen Lewis Brereton, released the first internal assessment on the mission and made four points:

1. Had the operation been executed as planned at least 90 per cent success would have been obtained and combat losses would have been minimized. Complete surprise was attained by the first elements to reach the objective, but defenses were thoroughly alerted by the time the last three groups arrived, thirty minutes later.

2. Complex operations of this nature require extreme precision and timing, and are most difficult to control and coordinate, especially when navigation must be conducted over great distances.

3. Anticipating that the enemy air warning system would pick up the formations after crossing the Danube, in any case, hindsight suggests that a decision to break radio silence and reassemble the entire formation at the Danube might have resulted in greater success and fewer losses.

4. The decision of the commander to execute an attack from the south after his formation had been lost and missed its IP was unsound. It resulted in wrong targets being bombed, destroyed coordination, and sacrificed the benefits of thorough briefing and training of the crews. Each individual crew had been assigned an individual target and trained to recognize it from models and photographs based on an approach from the northwest.

Although tactical errors and erroneous decisions are pointed out above, no blame is attached to any commander or leader participating in the mission for decisions which were made on the spot under the stress of combat. On the other hand, the IX Bomber Command is deserving of the highest praise for its excellent staff procedure and leadership displayed in the planning, training, and execution of this most difficult mission.

Brereton's assessment provides an interesting insight into Ninth Air Force's thinking at the time. It contains a fair number of dubious conclusions. Brereton's initial point that *Tidal Wave* would have accomplished 90 percent success if carried out as planned was unduly optimistic. As the 1944 oil campaign would demonstrate, the refineries were much more durable targets than was believed in 1943. It would take a sustained campaign against the refineries to significantly diminish their output for a prolonged period of time.

Compton's navigational error played the single largest role in derailing *Tidal Wave*. The failure to strike Targets White I through White III meant that *Tidal Wave* bombers hit only about half of the refining capacity they had been assigned to attack. Furthermore, the strike at

Several of the *Tidal Wave* senior commanders are seen here after the mission, with Col Leon Johnson of the 44th Group at the left and Col John "Killer" Kane of the 98th Group at the right receiving the highest American decoration, the Medal of Honor. Brig Gen Uzal Ent, in the center, was awarded the Distinguished Service Cross.

A photo taken a few days after *Tidal Wave* showing the group commanders. Left to right are Col Leon Johnson (44th Group); Maj George Brown (acting CO, 93rd Group), Col K. K. Compton (376th Group) and Col Jack Wood (389th Group). Col Kane from the 98th Group was still on Cyprus when this photo was taken.

the largest refinery, Astra Română, had poor results after the 93rd Group made its impromptu attack, thereby interfering with the attack by Kane's 98th Group as they weaved through the smoke and exploding bombs. Compton's 376th Group made no concerted attacks at all.

Compton's and Ent's rigid adherence to radio silence sacrificed their ability to exert command-and-control over the mission. The main purpose of radio silence was to minimize the risk of early warning of the *Tidal Wave* attack. As detailed earlier, this proved futile in the face of the Luftwaffe early warning network. Compton and Ent were unaware that the mission secrecy had been compromised almost from the start of the flight. When Bulgarian fighters were spotted in late morning, there should have been some inkling that the mission was being monitored. It is likely that Ent and Compton knew about the Bulgarian fighters since they were spotted by trailing formations. Under conditions of radio silence, these sightings were not reported to the lead flight.

This was far from the worst consequence of the rigid enforcement of radio silence. As Brereton suggested, breaking radio silence after crossing the Danube could have permitted Compton and Ent to herd all five groups together to attack simultaneously instead of in two separate waves. On the other hand, it begs the question whether a unified formation might not have followed Compton's navigational error, resulting in all five groups failing to bomb their intended targets.

Most disturbing was Compton and Ent's apparent decision to maintain radio silence after the final turn to target was made. Had they kept open the radio channel between "Teggie Ann" and the rest of the groups, Compton's navigation error might have been corrected promptly as Baker eventually corrected the 93rd Group.

Brereton apparently regarded Ent's errors as more serious than Compton's. Brereton was unhappy with Ent's earlier resistance of the *Tidal Wave* plan, and his leadership during the mission was questionable in many regards. Any public airing of his concerns over Ent's leadership would have undermined the public depiction of the success of the *Tidal Wave* mission. Instead, Ent was sent back to a training post in the United States. Although Brereton's assessment noted the costly navigational error, Compton was not singled out for this decision. Once again, a public rebuke of the mission leaders would have called into question the execution of the mission and this would have reflected on Brereton's judgments as well. Compton went on to become air chief of staff for operations, Fifteenth Air Force in March 1944 and later had a distinguished career in the postwar Air Force.

The next mission for the five *Tidal Wave* B-24 groups was Operation *Juggler*, an attack on the Messerschmitt airframe plant at Wiener Neustadt in Austria. Here, the 376th "Liberandos" are being briefed by Major Norman Appold, who led the only flight from the Liberandos to actually attack a refinery at Ploesti. Behind him is the group commander, Col K.K. Compton. This was the last major bomber mission for IX Bomber Command prior to the reorganization of the Mediterranean bomber force at the end of August 1943.

During the flight back to Benghazi, Compton suggested to Ent that they bring up Kane for court-martial due to the failure of his group to maintain contact with the lead groups, thereby violating the mission orders. Ent had the sense to quash this preposterous idea, reminding Compton that they had failed to follow mission orders as well due to the navigational error. Ent realized that their necks would be on the chopping block sooner than Kane's if the ugly notion of court-martial was raised.

In the event, both Kane and Johnson were singled out for their heroic leadership in executing their groups' attacks in the face of ferocious enemy resistance. Both were awarded the Medal of Honor with little or no dissent. The leaders of the 93rd Group, Lt Col Addison Baker and co-pilot Maj John Jerstad were nominated for the Medal of Honor for their heroic decision to attack Ploesti in spite of Compton's navigational error. There was some dissension over this nomination since they failed to follow the mission orders and attacked a target of opportunity instead. Nevertheless, it was hard to deny the heroism of their actions, and both were awarded the decoration posthumously. One pilot was singled out for recognition, Lt Lloyd Hughes, who had continued to carry out the attack on the target in spite of the fatal damage to his aircraft.

A total of 56 Distinguished Service Crosses were awarded to *Tidal Wave* crews, including Ent and Compton, along with 41 Silver Stars for valor. In view of the exceptionally high rate of casualties, the USAAF decided to award the Distinguished Flying Cross to all 1,320 crewmen who took part in the *Tidal Wave* mission. No other USAAF mission in World War II ever approached the number of decorations awarded for *Tidal Wave*.

The first full-scale assessment of Operation *Tidal Wave* was issued by the Office of the Assistant Chief of Staff, Intelligence, USAAF on September 30, 1943, two months after the mission. Allied reconnaissance missions over Ploesti, conducted mainly by RAF units, provided comprehensive photographic coverage of most of the facilities and allowed intelligence officers to plot most bomb impacts. This report estimated that *Tidal Wave* had shut down the equivalent of 75 percent of Ploesti capacity for a month and had destroyed 3.9 million tons of annual processing capacity or 46 percent of Ploesti's output for a period of six months or more. Destruction of storage facilities was believed to total 325,000 tons and assuming that these storage tanks were half full, the report estimated that about 162,000 tons of petroleum products had been destroyed. As time went on, these assessments were revealed to be wildly optimistic.

Suspicions about the conclusions of the September 1943 report began to emerge in late 1943 as it became evident that, in the months after *Tidal Wave*, Ploesti was continuing to refine crude oil at rates equal to or higher than before the strikes. Production at Ploesti fell from 407,000 tons in July 1943 to 269,000 tons in August, but had already rebounded to 431,000 tons in September 1943. A later Romanian report also indicated that the attacks destroyed only 50,000 metric tons of stored petroleum products rather than the 162,000 tons estimated by USAAF intelligence.

The fundamental flaw in the *Tidal Wave* plan was the failure to appreciate the enormous amount of reserve capacity in the Ploesti refinery system. Romanian crude oil production in 1943 was 5.3 million metric tons, but the Ploesti refineries had the capacity to process over 9.1 million metric tons. In other words, there was a 40 percent "cushion." In order to effectively reduce Romanian refined fuel output, the bombing attacks had to completely eliminate this cushion before any long-term decline in Romanian fuel deliveries would occur. The *Tidal Wave* attacks had reduced the Ploesti refinement capacity by only about 200,000 metric tons, so it barely dented the cushion. As a result, Ploesti output rebounded immediately in September 1943, since crude oil that would have gone to the disabled plants was simply shifted to other refineries. For example, the Astra Română refinery that had been missed by Compton's 376th Group refined 123,000 metric tons in July and increased this to 145,000 metric tons in September.

Although the IX Bomber Command had originally planned to conduct follow-on attacks against Ploesti if deemed necessary, these did not occur until the spring of 1944. To begin with, the *Tidal Wave* losses were so severe that any follow-on attacks would have been dangerously small. On August 2, 1943, the IX Bomber Command could muster only about 33 B-24D bombers for a follow-on mission since many of the bombers that had returned from *Tidal Wave* had suffered battle damage and others had engine problems. Over the next few months, the initial assessments of *Tidal Wave*'s apparent success dissuaded the IX Bomber Command from conducting additional costly missions against Ploesti. As a result, Ploesti was spared from further attacks until 1944 as described below.

The Axis perspective

In his initial report to Berlin, Gen Gerstenberg acknowledged the damage to the refineries, but noted that it would not appreciably diminish the supply of fuel to Germany and its allies. Furthermore, the US Army Air Force had suffered crippling losses from the attack. On August 3, 1943, the senior Romanian and German leadership held a conference in Bucharest to discuss the lessons from the Ploesti raid. The meeting included Marshal Ion Antonescu, General de escadră Gheorghe Jienescu (Romanian Air Minister), General de divizie Gheorghe D. Marinescu (Romanian Air Defenses), German Ambassador Manfred Freiherr von Killinger, Gen Alfred Gerstenberg (head of the Luftwaffe mission), Oberst Woldenga (German fighter forces), Gen Kuderna (commander of 5.Flak Division), and others.

Gerstenberg noted that even though the raid had caused considerable damage, the refineries were still operating and that production could be returned to normal in a few weeks. The Flak defense of Ploesti was judged to be the single most important factor in the defeat of the raid, though there were various suggestions for improving air defense. Ploesti and the Prahova valley had only about a third of the total Romanian and German antiaircraft artillery in Romania, and the conference felt that the Flak was too dispersed.

As a result, a program was initiated to concentrate the Flak defenses on the most critical locations including Bucharest, Ploesti, the Cernavoda bridge, the port of Constanţa, and the factory cities of Reşiţa and Braşov. There was also a general agreement over the need for more antiaircraft guns including heavy batteries of 105mm, due to the supposition that future raids would come from high altitudes after the failure of the low-altitude raid. Fighter forces would also have to be strengthened, and additional radar stations deployed for early warning.

In total, the FARR had 31 available aircraft with crews on August 1 and conducted 54 sorties, with 13 kill claims. The Luftwaffe had 26 aircraft with crews available near Ploesti, conducted 69 sorties, and claimed 15 kills. This does not count the further five kill claims by Jagdgeschwader.27 based at Kalamaki/Tanagara in Greece, which attacked the returning *Tidal Wave* force over the Ionian Sea.

Romanian assessments seriously downgraded the number of bombers lost to fighters. Part of the issue was that many of the bombers claimed by fighters had been fatally damaged by Flak, and the fighters merely arrived on the scene to deliver a *coup de grâce*. One of the main technical assessments after *Tidal Wave* was that the fighter aircraft had to be upgraded with 20mm cannon as the machine-gun-armed fighters could simply not do enough damage to a heavy bomber.

The *Tidal Wave* bomber crews claimed to have shot down 52 enemy aircraft, a substantial exaggeration. The Luftwaffe lost two BF 109G-2 fighters destroyed and four damaged from I./JG.4, and two Bf 109G destroyed and one damaged from JG.27 in the final encounters over the Ionian Sea. Night-fighter losses were one Bf 110E-4 destroyed and four damaged from NJG.6. The FARR lost two IAR 80 fighters and three damaged; one Romanian Bf 110C was also shot down. There were also at least two Romanian Bf 109G-2s damaged during the engagements.

Luftwaffe bomber claims, August 1, 1943			
Pilot	**Unit**	**Altitude**	**Time**
Oblt Hans-Wilhelm Schöpper	Stab I./JG 4	40m	12.00
Hptm Wilhelm Steinmann	Stab I./JG 4	300m	12.01
Hptm Hans Eder	Stab I./JG 4	100m	12.06
Lt Philipp Bouquet	3./JG 4	50m	12.07
Oblt Manfred Spenner	3./JG 4	30m	12.07
Lt Erwin Rauch	Stab I./JG 4	10–20m	12.09
Ofw Frank Gühl	2./JG 4	100–150m	12.11
Lt Werner Gerhartz	I./JG 4	50m	12.16
Fw Hans Maier	2./JG 4	100m	12.17
Uffz Kurt Rünge	2./JG 4	50m	12.20
Lt Günther Stark	1./JG 4	50m	12.20
Hptm Wilhelm Steinmann	Stab I./JG 4	50m	12.28
Uffz Jürgen Knäbel	10./NJG 6	10m	12.31
Uffz Jürgen Knäbel	10./NJG 6	10m	12.38–44
Ofw Georg Klever	10./NJG 6	10m	12.43
Fw Ernst Hackl	12./JG 27	1,000m	15.30
Oblt Ernst-Georg Altnorthoff	12./JG 27	2,000m	15.32
Uffz Rudolf Philipp	12./JG 27	1,000m	15.35
Oblt Alfred Burk	11./JG 27	2,000m	17.10
Lt Hans Flor	Stab IV./JG 27	1,200m	17.13

Romanian bomber claims, August 1, 1943			
Pilot	**Squadron**	**Aircraft**	**Kill claims**
Lt Ion Barladeanu	Esc. 45	IAR 80	2
Adj Ioan Nicola	Esc. 45	IAR 80	1
Lt Ion Maga	Esc. 53	Bf 109G	1
Adj Dumitru Encioiu	Esc. 53	Bf 109G	1
Lt Criste Cristu	Esc. 59	IAR 80	1
Adj Ioan Bosinceanu	Esc. 59	IAR 80	1
Lt Carol Anastasescu	Esc. 62	IAR 80	2
Adj Ilie Dumitru	Grupul 6	IAR 80	2
Adj Aurel Vladareanu	Grupul 6	IAR 80	1
Ad. Stefan Nicoară	Unknown	–	1

Romanian accounts indicate that 34–36 bombers were shot down over Romania, of which nine crashed within the immediate Ploesti area and 26 in areas away from the city. The varying numbers of bombers was due to the fact that several bombers disintegrated and burned after crashing into the refineries. In 1944, Romanian officials provided the US with a list of 25 of the aircraft that were relatively intact that could be identified by serial number. The accompanying map here, based on Romanian records, details 34 crash sites. Romanian assessments put the causes of the bomber losses to Flak (20), fighters (12), and balloon cables (4). The initial US assessment was that Flak was the major cause of losses over Ploesti, with fighters responsible for five or six losses, balloon cables one loss, and possibly one or two planes engulfed in bomb blasts or other ground conflagrations. Both the Germans and Romanians attributed most of the Flak kills to the light 20mm and 37mm guns. The 88mm guns were not well suited to engagements at low altitude. The Romanian Gendarmerie reported that the USAAF had suffered 214 dead in Romania, but also reported that some aircraft were so badly burned that crew remains were impossible to identify.

Flak employment around Ploesti August 1, 1944			
	Batteries	**Guns**	**Rounds expended**
Romanian 20mm/37mm	6	78	19,471
Romanian 88mm	15	68	1,452
German 20mm/37mm	10	132	36,800
German 88mm	21	96	2,100
Sub-total, 20mm/37mm	16	210	56,271
Sub-total 88mm	36	164	3,552
Totals	52	374	59,823

Casualty figures on the ground vary from report to report. Most contemporary reports indicate over 300 dead and wounded and the accompanying table provides one of the few detailed breakdowns between military and civilian casualties. The single most costly event was the B-24 crash into the women's penitentiary which caused 61 dead and 60 wounded. Equipment losses were three 88mm guns, and five 20mm guns. Seven barrage balloons were knocked free when their cables were severed and five more were set on fire and destroyed.

Casualties in Ploesti Area, August 1, 1943			
	Dead	**Wounded**	**Total**
German military	3	19	22
Romanian military	12	29	41
Romanian civilian	80	170	250
Total	95	218	313

Romanian reports of bomb impacts					
	Ploesti	**Câmpina**	**Brazi**	**Other**	**Total**
HE bombs	217	131	52	100	500
Failed to detonate	22	11	2		
Incendiaries	1,430	2,000	90	763	4,283
Failed to detonate	430	500	–	–	–

Return to Ploesti

Strategic decisions spared Ploesti from any further attacks until 1944. Under the Combined Bomber Offensive (CBO) plans, the principal mission for the USAAF's heavy bombers was the destruction of the Luftwaffe fighter force by attacks against the German aircraft industry. This campaign was codenamed Operation *Pointblank*.[1] The Ninth Air Force was assigned a role in these attacks, starting with Operation *Juggler* on August 13, 1943. This involved 114 B-24 bombers from Benghazi attacking the Messerschmitt airframe plant in Wiener Neustadt, south of Vienna.

The change in strategic focus occurred as organizational changes were disrupting the heavy bomber force in the Mediterranean theater. The three B-24 groups sent from the UK for *Tidal Wave* returned to the Eighth Air Force in Britain after Operation *Juggler*. Brereton's Ninth Air Force headquarters was shifted to Britain in October 1943 as part of the Operation *Overlord* build-up. In its place, the Fifteenth Air Force took over the heavy bomber mission in the Mediterranean Theater of Operations (MTO). It moved its bases from North Africa to Italy after the successful landings at Salerno in September 1943.

The Fifteenth Air Force, along with the Eighth Air Force based in Britain, constituted the United States Strategic Air Force (USSTAF) and was assigned to the *Pointblank* mission against the German aircraft industry. The focus of the Fifteenth Air Force attacks were plants that were more remote from the United Kingdom. This included factories in southern Germany and Austria.

The mission of the USSTAF did not begin to change until the spring of 1944 after the success of *Pointblank* in whittling down the Luftwaffe fighter force. In February 1944, Gen Carl Spaatz began preliminary steps to start a new campaign aimed at German oil. This was intended to wreck the main source of German fighter fuel, the synthetic fuel plants in Germany, but also other sources of fuel, namely the Romanian refineries. By late 1943, the Ploesti refineries were providing about a third of the Luftwaffe's high-octane fuel. This plan became tangled up in a series of controversies over the role of the heavy bomber force prior to the Operation *Overlord* landings in Normandy. Eisenhower insisted that the USSTAF shift the focus of its missions from the bombing campaign in Germany to missions in support of the forthcoming Operation *Overlord*.

1   Steven Zaloga, *Operation* Pointblank *1944: Defeating the Luftwaffe*, Campaign 236 (Oxford: Osprey, 2011).

In March 1944, the USSTAF Special Planning Committee recommended that the heavy bombers be used against the German fuel industry, especially sources of gasoline, as a means to cripple the mobility of the German army and Luftwaffe in the forthcoming Normandy campaign. Eisenhower's deputy, Air Chief Marshall Sir Arthur Tedder, felt that the German fuel industry was too substantial and would take too long to cripple before its effects would be felt on the battlefield. Tedder argued that the missions in April–May 1944 would be more productive in the short term if aimed at disrupting the railway network between Germany and France to prevent the *Wehrmacht* from reinforcing its forces near the beachhead. The principal targets for the heavy bombers were major bottlenecks in the railroad network, especially key bridges, tunnels, and marshalling yards. Tedder won Eisenhower's approval for this approach. Spaatz and his senior commanders continued to argue for the oil targets.

Besides the new emphasis on the *Overlord* missions, the USSTAF was directed by the Combined Chiefs of Staff to participate in the *Crossbow* campaign to preempt German missile attacks on Britain.[2] This further diluted the ability of the USSTAF from conducting missions into Germany. As a result of these two new assignments, the CCS were unwilling to sanction Spaatz's oil campaign in the early spring of 1944. The CCS did allow some attacks in Romania, for example, mining the Danube to cut off the main route of supply starting in April 1944. Other targets were added, including rail-to-barge trans-shipment points. The mining operation was carried out primarily by the RAF's 205 Group.

Regardless of the temporary delay in the start of the oil campaign, the Fifteenth Air Force began to take preliminary steps to return to Ploesti. In light of the horrific losses suffered in Operation *Tidal Wave*, the idea that the refineries could be eliminated by a single massive attack at low altitude was recognized as unrealistic. The only plausible alternative was a prolonged campaign from high altitude. This approach was not without its problems

For the June 10, 1944 dive-bombing mission against the Română American refinery, the P-38 Lightnings of the 82nd Fighter Group were modified to carry a 1,000lb bomb and a 300-gallon drop tank for the 1,250-mile round trip flight from Foggia, Italy to Ploesti.

2   Steven Zaloga, *Operation* Crossbow *1944: Hunting Hitler's V-Weapons*, Air Campaign 5 (Oxford: Osprey, 2018).

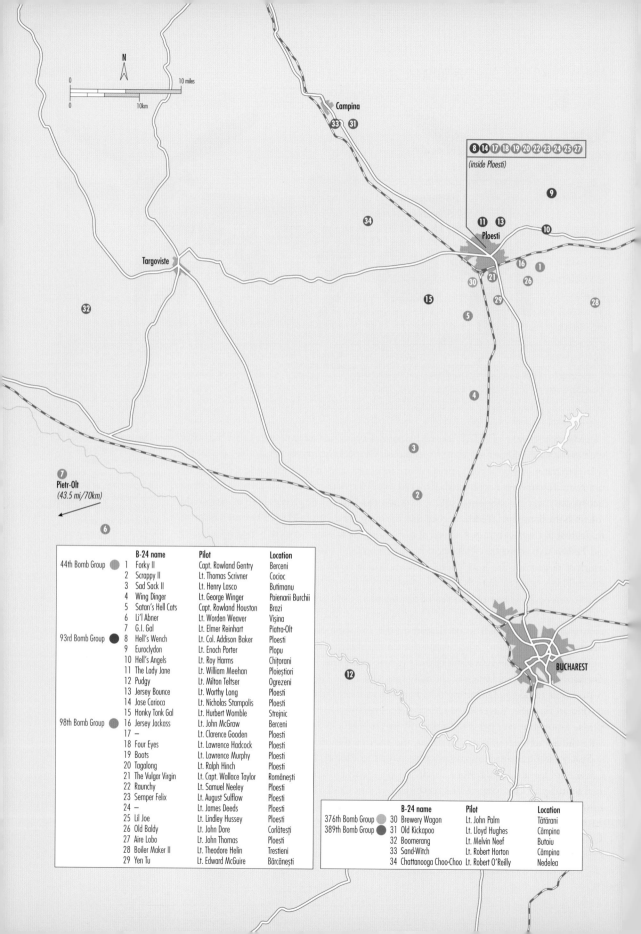

N

0   10 miles
0   10km

Campina

33 **31**

8 **14** **17** **18** **19** **20** **22** **23** **24** **25** **27**
(inside Ploesti)

9

34

11 **13**

Ploesti

10

16

1

30 **21**

26

29

28

Targoviste

32

15

5

4

3

2

7
Pietr-Olt
(43.5 mi/70km)

6

12

BUCHAREST

		B-24 name	Pilot	Location
44th Bomb Group	1	Forky II	Capt. Rowland Gentry	Berceni
	2	Scrappy II	Lt. Thomas Scrivner	Cocioc
	3	Sad Sack II	Lt. Henry Lasco	Butimanu
	4	Wing Dinger	Lt. George Winger	Poienarii Burchii
	5	Satan's Hell Cats	Capt. Rowland Houston	Brazi
	6	Li'l Abner	Lt. Worden Weaver	Vișina
	7	G.I. Gal	Lt. Elmer Reinhart	Piatra-Olt
93rd Bomb Group	8	Hell's Wench	Lt. Col. Addison Baker	Ploesti
	9	Euroclydon	Lt. Enoch Porter	Plopu
	10	Hell's Angels	Lt. Roy Harms	Chițorani
	11	The Lady Jane	Lt. William Meehan	Ploieștiori
	12	Pudgy	Lt. Milton Teltser	Ogrezeni
	13	Jersey Bounce	Lt. Worthy Long	Ploesti
	14	Jose Carioca	Lt. Nicholas Stampolis	Ploesti
	15	Honky Tonk Gal	Lt. Hurbert Womble	Strejnic
98th Bomb Group	16	Jersey Jackass	Lt. John McGraw	Berceni
	17	–	Lt. Clarence Gooden	Ploesti
	18	Four Eyes	Lt. Lawrence Hadcock	Ploesti
	19	Boots	Lt. Lawrence Murphy	Ploesti
	20	Tagalong	Lt. Ralph Hinch	Ploesti
	21	The Vulgar Virgin	Lt. Capt. Wallace Taylor	Românești
	22	Raunchy	Lt. Samuel Neeley	Ploesti
	23	Semper Felix	Lt. August Sulflow	Ploesti
	24	–	Lt. James Deeds	Ploesti
	25	Lil Joe	Lt. Lindley Hussey	Ploesti
	26	Old Baldy	Lt. John Dore	Corlătești
	27	Aire Lobo	Lt. John Thomas	Ploesti
	28	Boiler Maker II	Lt. Theodore Helin	Trestieni
	29	Yen Tu	Lt. Edward McGuire	Bărcănești

		B-24 name	Pilot	Location
376th Bomb Group	30	Brewery Wagon	Lt. John Palm	Tătărani
389th Bomb Group	31	Old Kickapoo	Lt. Lloyd Hughes	Câmpina
	32	Boomerang	Lt. Melvin Neef	Butoiu
	33	Sand-Witch	Lt. Robert Horton	Câmpina
	34	Chattanooga Choo-Choo	Lt. Robert O'Reilly	Nedelea

since high-altitude attacks were likely to be less accurate than low-altitude attacks, and a prolonged campaign would undoubtedly be confronted by reinforced German and Romanian air defenses.

In the wake of Operation *Tidal Wave*, Gerstenberg had indeed succeeded in reinforcing the defenses of the Romanian oil industry. The fighter force in the oil region was more than doubled to about 200–250 fighters. Likewise, the fighter defenses along the route into Romania in Serbia and Bulgaria had been increased to about 100 fighters. Flak defenses were also substantially improved, including the addition of heavier 105mm and 128mm Flak guns as well as more fire direction radars.

The Fifteenth Air Force hoped that several innovations would counterbalance the German defensive improvements. The introduction of new bomber radars, notably the APS-15 "Mickey," was expected to improve bombing accuracy from higher altitudes as well as to provide the capability to strike the refineries even when they were obscured by smoke or weather. As a result of the experiences during Operation *Pointblank*, the USSTAF was now supporting the bomber missions with a growing escort fighter force.

In early 1944, there were still shortcomings in the escort force supporting the Fifteenth Air Force. At this time, the principal escort fighters were the P-47 and P-38. The P-47 did not have adequate range for the Romanian mission. The P-38, though better suited to these missions, was still suffering performance problems such as lingering issues with the engine superchargers. However, by late spring, this situation improved dramatically with innovations such as improved drop tanks, and the arrival of the P-51 Mustang escort fighter.

In frustration over the CCS restrictions against the oil campaign, Spaatz decided to use bureaucratic subterfuge to begin it anyway by interpreting the requirements of the transportation missions in the broadest sense possible. The Fifteenth Air Force had a marginal role in both the preparations for *Overlord* and Operation *Crossbow* since the main focus of these missions was in northern France.

The USAAF returned to Ploesti with the first raid of the new year on April 5, 1944, conducted by the Fifteenth Air Force, Mediterranean Army Air Force (MAAF). Due to a lack of formal CCS approval, the early missions were reported as missions against the transportation infrastructure such as railway yards, not the refineries. An Army Air Forces Evaluation Board later justified this approach by noting that "The direction of flight… plus the compactness of the target area made bomb spillage in the refinery well nigh inevitable."

Tedder recognized that the Fifteenth Air Force could only plan a marginal role in the *Overlord* missions, and he began to acknowledge that missions against Ploesti might be more beneficial than sanctioned targets such as the Balkan communication infrastructure. Attacks on Ploesti through April 1944 were still categorized as attacks on the neighboring railway yards, although it became increasingly evident to the bomber crews that the real missions were the refineries.

Spaatz did not want to begin a full-blown campaign against Ploesti by the Fifteenth Air Force until the Eighth Air Force could join in with attacks against the German synthetic fuel industry in Germany. With the commitment to the preparation of *Overlord* winding down by mid-May 1944, the oil campaign began to pick up steam. On May 12, 1944 the Eighth Air Force conducted its first thousand-bomber raid on the German fuel industry in Germany, officially opening the oil campaign. By this stage Tedder and the CCS backed these missions, and the Fifteenth Air Force began its dedicated missions against the Ploesti refineries with missions in late May.

The German smoke generation system installed around Ploesti could be quite effective with the proper wind conditions, as is seen in this view from an unidentified mission in the summer of 1944.

On May 18 the mission was disrupted by poor weather and the planned attack by 700 bombers was reduced to only 206 B-17s and B-24s. On top of the weather, the smoke dischargers at Ploesti proved to be very effective in obscuring the refineries. The results of this attack were poor, with only eight bombs landing within the Română Americana facility. The May 26 raid was a night mission by 74 RAF bombers. The most successful mission in May took place on May 31 when the Fifteenth Air Force hit four refineries with 481 bombers. The Concordia Vega refinery was struck by 156 bombs, destroying the boiler house and putting the plant out of operation for more than two weeks. Română Americana was hit by 37 bombs, damaging the boiler house and crippling operations for a month.

Since the initial seven missions by heavy bombers from high altitude had failed to shut down the Ploesti refineries, Fifteenth Air Force decided to try a surprise low-level attack using P-38 Lightning fighters in a bomber role on June 10, 1944. The 82nd Fighter Group provided 46 fighters, each carrying a 1,000lb bomb and an extra drop tank. The 1st Fighter Group provided the escort. By the time it reached Ploesti, the P-38 bomber force was reduced to 38 aircraft due to the usual problem with aborts on long-range missions. On approaching Ploesti, the 1st Fighter Group became mixed up in a large number of dog-fights. The 1st Fighter Group claimed to have shot down 24 German and Romanian aircraft during the mission. The dive-bombing mission against the Română Americana refinery proved reasonably successful in view of the number of aircraft involved. A total of 25 bombs landed within the refinery, stopping production for about a week, but the losses on this mission were prohibitive. The 82nd Fighter Group lost ten of 38 P-38 fighter-bombers while the 1st Fighter Group lost 14 of the 21 P-38 fighters on escort duty. This was the first and last time this tactic was employed.

The summer campaign against Ploesti returned to a grinding, attritional struggle. Allied signals intelligence acquired growing evidence of the impact of the oil campaign on crippling the Luftwaffe, further reinforcing the commitment to these missions in general and the Ploesti effort in particular. The decrypted Luftwaffe messages made it very clear that the Luftwaffe in Normandy was restricting its aerial operations due to crippling fuel shortages. On June 8, Spaatz informed the Fifteenth Air Force that their number one priority would be the destruction of the Romanian oil refineries. By this point, about half of the 60 oil refineries in Romania and Hungary had been damaged or destroyed. The attacks in June and July were also extended to fuel infrastructure facilities such as storage and pipelines. The RAF continued mining operations along the Danube River as a means to block fuel exports from Romania to Germany.

The Luftwaffe and FARR remained vigorous and active in June 1944, for example conducting 198 fighter sorties against the June 23 mission. However, the USAAF escort fighters took a toll, with 24 German and Romanian fighters claimed that day in the vicinity of Ploesti, including the loss of two of four of the Romanian group commanders. In late June 1944, the Fifteenth Fighter Command changed its tactics, diverting some of the escort fighters to sweeps against the Romanian and German airfields. Aside from the growing losses to escort fighters, there was an increasing shortage of experienced Luftwaffe and Romanian fighter pilots. As a result, the strength

A B-24J of the 718th Squadron, 449th Group, Fifteenth Air Force flies over an enormous plume of smoke after an August 1944 mission over Ploesti.

of the German and Romanian fighter units continued to decline and, by late July, less than 50 fighters were active on a daily basis. For example, during the July 28 mission, only 48 fighters managed to get airborne, and the escorts kept all of these away from the bombers. This was a far cry from the 182 sorties directed against the first mission on April 5, 1944.

Flak defenses in the Ploesti area continued to increase from 142 heavy Flak guns in April 1944 to 253 guns by the summer of 1944. This formidable Flak defense was concentrated in an area only about 12 x 16 miles (19 x 26km) in size. Most of the 105mm and 128mm guns were rail-mobile on special platforms, permitting them to be shifted around the city where needed. The Flak batteries were provided with ample supplies of ammunition. On a typical mission, the July 22 raid, 212 guns fired a total of 46,000 rounds over a two-hour period. The Ploesti defenses still managed to inflict surprisingly heavy losses on occasion. For example, on the night of August 9, the RAF's 205 Group staged a night mission with 61 Wellington, Liberator, and Halifax bombers, losing 11 bombers to Flak and Axis night fighters, nearly a fifth of the force.

Ploesti Flak defenses, summer 1944		
Type	**Batteries**	**Guns**
75–76mm	9	36
88mm	53	153
105mm	10	40
128mm	6	24
Total	78	253

An assessment of the summer 1944 raids on Ploesti singled out the smoke defenses as uniquely effective in degrading the bomber attacks. In spite of the use of aircraft radars to assist in aiming through the smoke, the smoke clouds managed to obscure the targets well enough that a large portion of bombs failed to hit their intended targets. The Ploesti refineries covered a very large area and their most important structures such as distillation and cracking plants were scattered about the sites and shielded by blast walls. For example, the Română Americana refinery covered some 131 acres but the vital targets within the refinery only amounted to 2.7 acres. The bomber attacks required considerable precision to cripple the production facilities, and the smoke generators proved unexpectedly efficient in interfering with the bombardier's aiming.

Bomber tactics against the refineries continued to evolve. The German Flak defenses were degraded by the use of chaff against the fire direction radars. The German smoke defenses had finite resources of chemicals to generate their smoke clouds. Instead of attacking in single massed formations, bomber wings attacked in sequence, eventually exhausting the smoke screens. In August, the bomber attacks were preceded by P-38 weather reconnaissance aircraft which remained on station as successive bomber wings conducted their bomb runs. The P-38s observed the smoke screens, and redirected the bombers to targets where the winds had cleared the smoke, or where the smoke emitters had run out of fuel.

Nevertheless, American bomber tactics were later faulted by Romanian and German Flak commanders. In an October 1944 meeting of USAAF officers and Romanian air defense commanders, the Romanians pointed out the shortcomings of the Fifteenth Air Force approach:

Our defense problem was simplified by your stereotyped method of attack. Your altitudes of attack were always from 6,000 to 8,000 meters (6,500–8,700ft). We always knew, within a half-hour, the time when you would attack. After you passed the [Initial Point], you made a long, straight bomb run for the target. There were no feints or evasive action or deviation. We had ideal conditions for target engagement and we took advantage of them… Under worst conditions we had at least a 25-minute warning. Normally we had at least 40 minutes to one hour…You almost always attacked when weather conditions were favorable to our defense and optical ranging.

To deal with the jamming of the fire-direction radars, the Ploesti defenders came up with other approaches to determine the exact altitude of the incoming American bombers. The Luftwaffe had reconditioned four captured US bombers, codenamed "Thistles," that would fly alongside the American formations, reporting to the Flak commanders about their altitude and speed.

The 1944 air campaign against Ploesti never managed to completely shut off the supply of refined petroleum, but it did dramatically reduce the flow to Germany. Refined fuel production at Ploesti had totaled 269,000 tons monthly prior to the 1944 bombing campaign. By May, it fell to 120,000 tons and by August to 84,000 tons. By early August 1944, the Ploesti refinery system had been shattered and the loss of infrastructure had made it nearly impossible to ship their petroleum products to Germany. As can be seen on the accompanying chart, only a fraction of the Ploesti output could actually be shipped to Germany due to the destruction of the rail and river transportation network. The final four raids were staged on August 17–19, shortly before the capture of Ploesti by the Red Army.

Fuel exports from Romania (in thousands of metric tons)			
Month	**Ploesti total crude oil throughput**	**Aviation gasoline to Luftwaffe**	**Gasoline to the Wehrmacht**
Dec '43	419	15	68
Jan '44	406	14	56
Feb '44	385	16	70
Mar '44	370	16	58
Apr '44	173	8	35
May '44	162	8	26
Jun '44	78	2	17
Jul '44	184	7	20
Aug '44	122	0.3	12

From April to August 1944, there were a total of 6,564 bomber sorties of which 5,229 reached and bombed their objectives. In addition, RAF bombers conducted three night missions on June 26–27, August 9–10, and August 17–18, totaling 186 sorties and dropping 313 tons of bombs at a cost of 19 bombers.

The 1944 air campaign against Ploesti revealed the basic flaw at the heart of the Operation *Tidal Wave* plan. It was naive to believe that a single mission could inflict sufficient damage on the Ploesti refineries. It took a sustained campaign over the course of several months to cripple the Romanian fuel facilities.

Fifteenth Air Force Ploesti Missions, 1944						
1944	**B-17 sorties***	**B-24 sorties***	**Total**	**Tonnage on target**	**Bomber losses**	**Escort fighter losses**
Apr 5	94	136	230	587.3	13	2
Apr 15	137	43	180	316.4	3	
Apr 24	154	136	290	793.5	8	3
May 5	166	319	485	1,256.5	19	1
May 18	33	173	206	493	14	2
May 31	53	428	481	1,115.6	16	4
Jun 6	–	310	310	697.5	14	–
Jun 10	38**	–	38	18.5	10	14
Jun 23	139	–	139	283.2	–	7
Jun 24	–	135	135	329	14	1
Jul 9	122	109	231	605	1	–
Jul 15	153	451	604	1,480.7	20	2
Jul 22	132	327	459	1,234.7	25	3
Jul 28	102	222	324	841.7	20	5
Jul 31	154	–	154	434.7	2	–
Aug 10	124	218	342	780.4	15	1
Aug 17	–	245	245	534.2	19	1
Aug 18	148	125	273	628.5	7	–
Aug 19	65	–	65	144.2	2	1
Total	1,776+ 38**	3,377	5,191	12,574.6	222	47
* Only effective sorties are tallied; aircraft returning to base and failing to bomb are not counted ** P-38 attack						

FURTHER READING

There have been numerous books about Ploesti over the years, many of which are cited here. The Dugan and Stewart book remains the classic account, and is still a valuable resource since the authors conducted numerous interviews with survivors from all sides through the 1960s. The later editions of the Way/Sternfels book are useful because Sternfels, pilot of "The Sandman" on the *Tidal Wave* mission, was able to conduct a number of candid interviews with participants in the early 2000s, including a rare conversation with "K. K." Compton. Stout's book provides a broader look at the attacks on Ploesti, covering not only the August 1943 raid but the subsequent 1944 campaign as well. Freeman's book in the "After the Battle" series provides a data-filled, visually rich record of *Tidal Wave*.

There have been a number of Romanian accounts of the battle, of which the recent Avram book is the most thorough. There are a number of articles on Romanian air defense in some of the specialist Romanian military journals. The special issue of the French aviation magazine *Batailles aeriennes* on Ploesti has the best account in print of the German/Romanian fighter forces during Operation *Tidal Wave*. There does not appear to be any book devoted to the German aspects of the Ploesti raid. The National Archives and Records Administration II in College Park, Maryland, has portions of the records of the Luftwaffe Mission to Romania in the RG 242 microfilm collection, but the documents peter out after 1941. The US Strategic Bombing Survey did not do a report on Ploesti, but the USSBS files in RG 243 at NARA II do include some significant material collected on this subject. The USAAF mission to Romania in 1944 collected a great deal of material related to the 1944 bombing campaign, but was unable to gather as much information on the 1943 *Tidal Wave* raid. This was due to the dispersal of many senior commanders, and the capture and imprisonment of leading German commanders, including Gerstenberg, by the Red Army. It's worth noting that the two studies cited below on German signals intelligence were not declassified by the NSA until 2009–14, which has led to some serious misunderstandings over the years about how the Luftwaffe was able to track *Tidal Wave*.

Government reports

n.a., *European Axis Signal Intelligence in World War II, Volume 5: The German Air Force Signal Intelligence Service*, Army Security Agency, May 1, 1946

n.a., *The Ploesti Mission of 1 August 1943*, US Air Force Historical Study No. 103, Historical Division, Assistant Chief of Air Staff, June 1944

n.a., *Ploesti*, Army Air Force Evaluation Report Volume VI, Mediterranean Theater of Operations, December 15, 1944

Praun, Gen Lt Albert, *German Radio Intelligence*, Foreign Military Studies P-038, HQ European Command, March 1950

Unga, Maior Constantin, *Referatul asupra bombardamentului American efectuat la 1 august 1943 asupra zonei petrolifere Ploeşti*, Inspectoratul General al Jandarmeriei, 1944

Books

Avram, Valeriu, and Armă, Alexandru, *Infern Deasupra Ploeieștiului: Bombardamentaul American de la 1 August 1943*, Editura Militară, Bucharest: 2012

Axworthy, Mark, et al., *Third Axis, Fourth Ally: Romanian Armed Forces in the European War 1941–1945*, Arms & Armour (London, 1994)

Bradle, William, *The Daring World War II Raid on Ploesti*, Pelican (Gretna, LA, 2016)

Brereton, Lewis, *The Brereton Diaries*, William Morrow (New York, 1946)

Brinzan, Radu, *The IAR.80 & IAR.81: Airframe, Systems & Equipment*, SAM Publications (Bedford, UK, 2011)

Buzatu, Gh., *A History of Romanian Oil, Volume 2*, Mica Valahie, (Bucharest, 2011)

Clendenin, Edward, *The Other Doolittle Raid*, Deeds (Athens, GA, 2017)

Cooke, Ronald, and Nesbit, Roy, *Target: Hitler's Oil, The Allied Attacks on German Oil Supplies 1939–45*, William Kimber (London, 1985)

Craven, Wesley, and Cate, James, *The Army Air Forces in World War II, Volume 2, Europe: Torch to Pointblank*, Office of Air Force History (Washington DC, 1983)

DiNardo, Richard, *Germany and the Axis Powers: From Coalition to Collapse*, University Press of Kansas (Lawrence, 2005)

Dugan, James, and Stewart, Carroll, *Ploesti: The Great Ground-Air Battle of 1 August 1943*, Potomac Books (Dulles, VA, 2002)

Ehlers, Robert, Jr, *Targeting the Third Reich: Air Intelligence and the Allied Bombing Campaign*, University Press of Kansas (Lawrence, 2009)

Eichholtz, Dietrich, *War for Oil: The Nazi Quest for an Oil Empire*, Potomac Books (Dulles, VA, 2012)

Freeman, Roger, *The Ploesti Raid: Through the Lens*, After the Battle (London, 2004)

Hill, Michael, *Black Sunday: Ploesti*, Schiffer (Atglen, PA, 1993)

Hill, Michael, *The Desert Rats: The 98th Bomb Group and the August 1943 Ploesti Raid*, Pictorial Histories (Missoula, MT, 1990)

Khazanov, Dmitriy B., *1941, Voyna v vozdukhe: Gorkiy uroki*, Yauza (Moscow, 2006)

Mackay, Ron, and Adams, Steve, *The 44th Bomb Group in World War II*, Schiffer (Atglen, PA, 2003)

Nedialkov, Dimitar, *B'lgarski iztrebiteli: Bulgarian Fighters, Volume 2*, Propeler (Sofia, 2006)

Pearton, Maurice, *Oil and the Romanian State*, Oxford University Press (Oxford, 1971)

Preda, Gavriil, et al., *Festung Ploiești*, Editura Printeuro (Ploesti, 2004)

Price, Alfred, *The History of US Electronic Warfare, Volume 1: The Years of Innovation – Beginning to 1946*, Association of Old Crows (Washington DC, 1984)

Stout, Jay, *Fortress Ploesti: The Campaign to Destroy Hitler's Oil*, Casemate (Haverton, PA, 2003)

Way, Frank, and Sternfels, Robert, *Burning Hitler's Black Gold*, Self-published, 6th Edition (2002)

Wilson, Paul, and Mackay, Ron, *The Sky Scorpions: The Story of the 389th Bomb Group in World War II*, Schiffer (Atglen, PA, 2006)

Articles

Carlson, Mark, "Heroes in Hell – What Really Happened at Ploesti," *Aviation History* (March 2012)

Cony, Christophe, et al., "Ploiesti: 1er août 1943," *Batailles aeriennes*, Special Number 25 (Jul–Sep 2003)

DiNardo, Richard, "The German Military Mission to Romania 1940–1941," *Joint Forces Quarterly*, Issue 69, 2 (2013), pp. 92–98

Dugan, James, and Stewart, Carroll, "Ploesti: German Defenses and Allied Intelligence," *The Air Power Historian*, Vol. 9, No. 1 (January, 1962), pp. 1–20

Iordache, Ioan, "Începuturile radarului în România: Cu ochii scrutând cerul în bezna nopții," *Modelism International*, No. 4 (2005), pp. 16–22

Munteanu, Col Dr Ioan, et al., "Evoluția artilleriei şi rachetelor antiaeriene," *Gândirea militară românească*, No. 3 (2016), pp.123–34.

n.a., "German Radar and US Countermeasures: What the 15th AF learned over Ploesti," *Radar*, No. 8 (February 1945), pp. 38–41

Neagoe, Gen Maj Dr Visarion, "Participarea artileriei antiaeriene în campaniile militare desfăşurate în perioda August 1943–23 August 1943," *Document: Buletinul arhivelur militare rômane*, Vol. 1 (55) (2012), pp. 61–73

Reese, John, "HALPRO: The Halverson Detachment in the Middle East June–July 1942," *Air Power History* (Summer 2010), pp. 32–43.

Rust (ed), Kenn, "The War Diary of John R. 'Killer' Kane: Out in the Blue," *AAHS Journal*, Part 3: Vol. 28 No. 1 (Spring 1983); Part 4: Vol. 28 No. 2 (Summer 1983)

Whelan, Norman, "Ploesti: Group Navigator's Eye View," *Aerospace Historian* (Spring, March 1976), pp. 1–6

INDEX

aircraft
  Avia B.354 "Dogan" 29, 43–44, **44**
  Bf 109/110 25, 26, 43–44, **58**
  IAR 80/81 **23**, 25, **25**, **26**, 49,
    56–57, 73–74
  P-38 **85**, 87, 90
  P-47 87
  Polikarpov I-16 Tip 24 **5**
  Zveno-SPB **5**
  see also B-24D
Alnorthoff, Oberstleutnant Ernst-Georg
  73, 75
Anestasescu, Lt Carol 55–58, **56–57**
antiaircraft defenses
  in action 48
  description 14–25, **17**, **18**, **19**, 37,
    87, 89
  Flak trains **20**, 21–23, 59
  maps **16**, **22**
  performance assessed 81–83
  see also barrage balloons; smoke gen-
    erators
Antonescu, Marshal Ion 14, 21, **24**, 81
Appold, Lt Norman 11, 51, 52, **80**
armament
  AAA 14–25, **17**, **18**, **19**, **20**, 89
  aircraft **11**, 13, **56–57**
Arnold, Gen "Hap" 30, 35
Astra Română refinery **5**, 58, 59, **59**, **62**,
  63, **64**, 78–79, 81

B-24D
  (42-40619) **70**
  (42-40743) **71**
  "Aire Lobo" 62
  "Available Jones" 75
  "Avenger" 67
  "Baby" 63
  "Bewitching Witch" (41-24042) **74**,
    75
  "Black Magic" **58**
  "Black Maria II" (41-11593) **7**
  "Boiler Maker II" 62
  "Boomerang" 72
  "Boots" 62
  "Brewery Wagon" (41-24294) 38–39,
    50, **51**
  "Chattanooga Choo-Choo" 71
  "Chug-a-Lug" (41-11766) 59, 62, **62**
  "Chum-V" (41-11630) **38**, **41**
  "Cornhusker" (42-40322) **73**, 75
  "Daisy Mae" **58**
  "Desert Lilly" (41-24258) 38, **51**
  "Doodlebug" (41-23724) **39**
  "Dopey Goldberg" **38**
  "Euroclydon" 55
  "Exterminator" **74**
  "Four Eyes" 62
  "G.I. Gal" 67–70
  "G.I. Ginnie" 51

"Hadley's Haven" **75**
"Hail Columbia" 36, 59, 63, 74
"Hell's Angels" 58
"Hell's Wench" 54–55
"Here's to Ya" 75
"Honkey Tonk Gal" 58
"Jerk's Natural" **66**
"Jersey Bounce 2nd" 49, 58
"Jersey Jackass" 63
"Joey Uptown" **38**
"Jose Carioca" 55
"Kickapoo" 38
"The Lady Jane" 55–58
"Lemon Drop" (41-23699) 67, **70**
"Let 'er Rip" 74
"Li'l Deucer" 58
"Lil Joe" 62
"Li'l Jughead" **58**
"Lorraine" (41-11591) **9**, **11**
"Margie" 62
"Nightmare" 62
"Old Baldy" 62
"Ole Kickapoo" 71–72
"Prince Charming" 74
"Pudgy" 58
"Raunchy" (41-11819) 59, **63**
"Ripper 1st" (41-11614) **6**
"Sand-Witch" 72
"The Sandman" **59**, 62
"Satan's Hell Cats" 67, **68–69**
"The Scorpion" 71
"Semper Felix" 63
"Snow White and the Seven Dwarves"
  (42-40364) **46–47**, **73**, 74
"The Squaw" (41-11761) **63**
"Strawberry Bitch" (42-72843) **10**
"Suzy Q" **64**, 65
"Tagalong" **58**, 59
"Teggie Ann" (42-40664) 38, 40, **41**,
  42, 45, 51, **76**
"Todelao" 72
"Utah Man" (41-24226) **66**
"Victory Ship" 66
"Vulgar Virgin" 62–63
"Wash's Tub" (41-11636) 11, **11**
"Wing Dinger" 64–65
"The Witch" **46–47**, 74
"Wongo Wongo" (42-40563) 38–40,
  42
"Yen Tu" 63
Baker, Lt Col Addison 13, 52, 54–55, 80
Barladeanu, Ioan 65–66
Barnett, Edward 65
barrage balloons **14**, 24, 37, 48, 83
Bleyer, Lt Col Julian 62
Bochev, Lt Petar 73
Bock, Lt James 11
bomb specifications 13, **85**
Bonev, Petr 74
Bosinceanu, av. 62

Bouquet, Leutnant Philipp 50–51
Brazi 12, 66–71, **67**, **68–69**
Brereton, Maj Gen Lewis 13, 31, 35–37,
  76, 77–78, 79
Brooks, Maj John **70**
Brown, Maj George **79**
Bucharest 14, 49, 50, 52
Bulgarian air force 29, 33, 43–44, **44**,
  73–74

Caldwell, Capt Kenneth 71
cameras, on-board **12**
Câmpina refinery
  attack on 11, 12, 33, 45, 52, 71–72,
    72
  defenses 17, 19
Carpenter, Lt Reginald **74**, 75
casualties 75–76, 77, 82–84, 91
Chica, Cpt. av. Marin 72
Colombia Aquila refinery 54, 55, 58,
  64–66, **64**, **65**
Compton, Col Keith K. **10**, **40**, **76**, **79**,
  80
  attitude to flying methods 13
  background and character 9, 11
  and the campaign 33, 38, 39–40, 43,
    44–45, 49, 50, 51, 52
  performance assessed 78–80
Concordia Vega refinery 51, 52, 59, **77**, 88
crash sites **86**
Creditul Minier refinery 52, 64, 66–71, **67**
Cristu, av. Criste 62

Daskalov, Lt 44
decoys 17–18
Deeds, Lt James 63
Dore, Lt John, Jr 62
Dufour, Lt Jerome **41**
Dumitrescu, Lt Mircea **25**

Ellis, Lt Lewis **58**
Encioiu, av. Dumitru 67
Ent, Brig Gen Uzal **10**, **40**, **76**, **78**
  and the campaign 38, 39, 51, 77
  performance assessed 79–80
  and plans 13, 36–37

fighter defenses 25–26, 87, 89
Flavelle, Lt Brian 11, 33, 38–40
Flor, Leutnant Hans 75

Gerstenberg, Generalmajor Alfred 20–21,
  26, 81, 87
Gheorghiu, Ermil **24**
Gooden, Lt Clarence 62
Graf, Uffz Max 75
Gunn, Capt James, III 73

Hackl, Fw Ernst 75
Hadcock, Lt Lawrence 62

Hadley, Lt Gilbert **75**
HALPRO mission (1942) 6–7, **6**, **7**, 20, 31
Halverson, Col Harry 6, 7
Harms, Lt Roy 58
Havens, Sgt Lycester 49
Helin, Lt Ted 62
Hinch, Lt Ralph **58**, 59
Horton, Lt Robert 72
Houston, Capt Rowland 67, **68–69**
Hughes, Lt Lloyd "Pete" 71–72, 80
Hussey, Lt Lindsey 62

Imperator network 21, **22**, 26–29, 48
Iovine, Lt Guy 38, 51

Jäfu Rumänien 27–28, 40–42, 44, 48, 49
Jägerleit Stellung Oktavien 27–28, **28**, **29**
Jerstad, Maj John 55, 80
Johnson, Col Leon 13, 64, **78**, **79**, 80
Jones, Lt Fred 75
Jordan, TSgt William **39**

Kane, Lt Col John "Killer" **78**
    attitude to flying methods 13
    background and character 9
    and the campaign 39, 43, 44, 59, 74
    performance assessed 80
Kendall, Lt Howard 66
Korger, Lt Harold 36–37
Krystev, Kristo 74
Kuderna, Generalmajor Julius 21, 81

Lasco, Lt Henry 65–66
Lawson, SSgt 72
Lebrecht, Lt Royden 63
Long, Lt Worthy 49, 58
Love, William 50
Luftwaffe
    5. Flak-Division 21, 23, 24, 25
    Flak-Regt,180 17, 19, 20, 21, 25, 48
    Flakgruppe Ploesti 15, **17**, 19, 25, 48
    Flakgruppe Vorfeldschutz (Băicoi)
        15–17, 19, 25
    JG.4 26, 48–49, 50–51, 52, 64, 67, 82
    NJG.6 26, 49, 82
    performance assessed 82–83
    role in defenses 17–26, 87, 89

Maga, Lt. Ion 67
maintenance 13
McAtee, Lt John 39, **40**
McBride, Maj Ralph 75
McCarty, Lt Ned 73, 75
McGraw, Lt John 63
McGuire, Lt Edward 63
Meehan, Lt William 55
Merrick, Lt 58
Morgan, Lt Leroy 62, **62**
Murphy, Lt Lawrence 62

navigational aids 12–13
Neef, Lt Melvin 72
Neeley, Lt Samuel 59, **63**
Nicholson, Lt **58**

oil
    losses due to attacks 63, 66, 70–71,
        72, 80–81, 90–91

Ploesti production statistics 30
Ploesti refineries overview 30
    strategic importance 4
Operation *Juggler* (1943) **80**, 84
Operation *Tidal Wave* (1943)
    battle scenes **46–47**, **56–57**, **68–69**
    low- vs high-altitude attack 13,
        35–37, **48**, 49–50
    radio silence issue 40, 43, 44–45, 78,
        79
O'Reilly, Lt Robert 71
Orion refinery 5, 63

Palm, Lt John 38–39, 50
Patch, Lt Dwight **58**
Philipp, Uffz Rudolf 75
Philips, Capt Reginald 67, **70**
Pitcairn von Perthshire, Oberstleutnant
    Douglas 28, 41, 44, 48, 49, 52
Ploesti **4**, **31**
    early attacks on 4–7
    later attacks on 81, 84–91
Porter, Lt Enoch, Jr 55
Posey, Lt Col Jim 52, 64, 66

radar 20–21, **22**, 27–28, **28**, **29**, 37, 48
    bomber radars 87
    gun-laying 21, **49**, 87, 90
radio monitoring 21, **22**, 26–29, 40–42
RAF 12, 80, 85, 88, 89, 91
Reinhart, Lt Elmer 67–70
Română Americana refinery 54, 88, 90
Romanian air force
    Esc. 45 25, 26, 48–49, 52, 65
    Esc. 51 26, 49
    Esc. 53 26, 48–49, 67
    Esc. 59 **23**
    Esc. 61 25, **25**, 26
    Esc. 62 25, 26, 55–58, **56–57**
    fighting abilities 25
    Grupul 6 **23**, 25, **25**, 48–49, 52
    performance assessed 82–83
Romanian army 14–17, **16**, 20, 24, 25, 48

Sabin, Capt Jesse **12**
Schöpper, Oberleutnant Hans-Wilhelm 50
Sisson, Lt Dab 71
Smart, Col Jacob 13, **30**, 31–35, 36–37,
    38
smoke generators 24, **27**, 48, 88, **88**, 90
Soviet Union 5–6, 18, 31, 35
Spaatz, Gen Carl 84, 85, 87, 89
Stampolis, Lt Nicolas 55
Standard Petrol Block refinery 58–59, **64**
Steaua refinery 71–72, **72**
Steinmann, Hauptmann Wilhelm 50, 67,
    68–69
Sternfels, Lt Robert 39–40, **59**
Stewart, Lt Walter **66**
Stoyanov, Por. Stoyan 74
Sulflow, Lt August 63

Tamulewicz, SSgt Joseph **39**
tanks, fuel 13, **85**
Taylor, Capt Wallace 62–63
Tedder, Air Chief Marshal Arthur 31, 35,
    85, 87
Teltser, Lt Milton 58

Thomas, Lt John 62
Thompson, Capt Ralph "Red" **40**, 45
Timberlake, Col E. J. 9, 13
training 11–13
trains *see* antiaircraft defenses: Flak trains

Unirea Sperantza refinery 59
USAAF 1st Fighter Group 88
USAAF 44th Group
    attack vectors **16**
    background 9
    and the campaign 23, 43, 44, 45,
        46–47, 52, 64–71, **67**, 75
    targets and strength 13, **31**, 36
USAAF 82nd Fighter Group 88
USAAF 93rd Group
    attack vectors **16**
    background 10
    and the campaign 43, 44, 45, 49, 50,
        51, 52, 54–59, **54**, 66, 74, 75
    performance assessed 79
    targets and strength 13. **31**, 36
USAAF 98th Group
    attack vectors and formation **16**, **60**
    background 9
    and the campaign 23, 38, 43, 44, 45,
        46–47, 52, **58**, 59–64, 74, 75
    list of members and fates 61
    performance assessed 79
    targets and strength 13, **31**, 36
USAAF 376th Group
    attack vectors **16**
    background 9, 11
    and the campaign 38–39, **38**, **39**, **41**,
        43, 44, 45, 49, 50–51, **51**, 52
    later campaigns 80
    performance assessed 79
    targets and strength 13, **31**, 36
USAAF 389th Group
    background 10–11
    and the campaign 43, 44, 45, 52,
        71–72
    targets and strength 13, 36
USAAF 449th Group **89**

Vaptsarov, Lt 44

W-Leit Südost 26–27, 29, 40
Ward, Capt Emery **70**
Weaver, Worden 64
Weisler, Lt Francis 63
Whitener, Lt Cecil 72
Whitney, Lt Col C. V. 31, 35
Wicklund, Capt Harold 38, 40, 45
Winger, Lt George 64–65
Woldenga, Oberstleutnant Bernhard 28,
    81
Womble, Lt Hubert 58
Wood, Col Jack 13, 52, 71, **79**
Wright, Lt William 50

Young, Lt John 39

Zimmerman, Lt William **9**